How to *Talk*
So Your Husband
Will *Listen*

How to *Talk* So Your Husband Will *Listen*

And *Listen* So Your Husband Will *Talk*

RICK JOHNSON

Revell

a division of Baker Publishing Group
Grand Rapids, Michigan

© 2008 by Rick Johnson

Published by Revell
a division of Baker Publishing Group
P.O. Box 6287, Grand Rapids, MI 49516-6287
www.revellbooks.com

ISBN 978-0-8007-2084-1

Previously published under the title *The Man Whisperer*

Printed in the United States of America

The Library of Congress has cataloged the original edition as follows:
Johnson, Rick, 1956–
    The man whisperer : speaking your man's language to bring out his best / Rick
Johnson.
        p.   cm.
    Includes bibliographical references.
    ISBN 978-0-8007-3197-7 (pbk.)
        1. Marriage—Religious aspects—Christianity. 2. Man-woman relationships—
Religious aspects—Christianity. 3. Communication in marriage. 4. Communication—
Sex differences. 5. Husbands—Psychology. I. Title.
BV835.J64 2008
248.8′435—dc22   2007052711

13   14   15   16   17   18   7   6   5   4   3   2

Dedicated to my lovely
(and influential) bride,
Suzanne.

Contents

Acknowledgments

I'd like to acknowledge all the great women out there who helped me with this book by giving me insight into the mysterious, complicated, and sometimes scary minds of the female gender—you know who you are.

I would also like to give a big thanks to Becky Johnson for her inspiration and key insights for this book.

The influence of applied femininity is, by any measure, incredibly determinative. In every culture, in every age, the power is awesome. And dangerous. As with any significant reservoir of power it may be used for good or ill. Its impact may be constructive or destructive. Like a mighty river, it is a force that may turn the turbines and generate power that will light up a community, a home, and a man's whole life. But undisciplined and unchecked, it may devastate, demoralize, and utterly destroy.

Some women have no clue how much actual power they hold, and those are the women who destroy their husbands by default. Other women are acutely aware of their power and make a conscious decision to become high controllers. But still other women, keenly aware of the power God has vested in their femininity, make a deliberate choice to use that power only for good.

Stu Weber, *Four Pillars of a Man's Heart*

1

A Woman's Whisper

> A woman can so easily crush a man's spirit. With a look. With a word. With a shrug of indifference.... Her cynicism is utterly emasculating, and many times, incredibly subtle. Like a fine, thin blade it slices deep, penetrating to the very core of his masculine soul.
>
> Stu Weber, *Four Pillars of a Man's Heart*

What is the difference between a traditional "horse trainer" and a "horse whisperer"? The difference is that a whisperer gets a PhD in the animal, studies the animal, and communicates in the animal's language rather than trying to get the animal to become more like a person.

The trainer simply demands the horse comply and fit into his world. In essence the trainer creates an obedient, castrated, brow-beaten pet. Some men married a long while to ultra-controlling women can relate to these geldings. Stallions are often castrated to make them more gentle and compliant. But it takes away their fire and passion for life and leadership. Stallions, not geldings, lead herds. Just like men, not geldings, lead families. (I know, mares actually lead the herd, but I'm taking liberty to make a point here.)

Some women have been forced to be leaders in their homes either through being a single mom or by living with a passive, apathetic man. But other women have wrested the mantle of leadership away from their men and clung to it tenaciously like a prized trophy. Either way it tends to castrate masculinity. And castrated masculinity is never healthy masculinity.

The horse whisperer, however, quietly observes and listens, and notes, and then gently enters the animal's world to make contact that is full of trust, rather than fear. The horse whisperer is compassionate, wise, and tender, yet firm. The result? An animal who trusts the whisperer, because the whisperer respects the animal. They form a pleasant, mutually giving relationship, and the horse and rider are both better for it.

The old song "Why Can't a Woman Be More Like a Man?" from *My Fair Lady* can be turned around to say, "Why Can't My Man Be More Like a Woman?"—which is subconsciously what many women are asking. It is the wrong question. The right question is, "How can I get a PhD in my man, so that I know how to encourage him to be his personal best self?"

Nearly every woman I talk to in connection with our Better Dads ministry eventually asks me some variation of the same question, "How can I change my man?" Generally it's phrased something like, "My husband is driving me crazy with [you fill in the blank]. How can I get him to stop?" In fact, the most frequent complaint men have about women is that women are always trying to change them. (The most frequent complaint women have about men is that men don't listen.) Unfortunately, the real question isn't *how* can a woman change a man but *can* a woman change a man? The answer from every man I ask this question to is, in a word . . . no.

On the surface it might appear that a woman can change a man. My uncle was a man fraught with demons of drink and deed for much of his youth, spending a significant amount of his adult life in prison. Upon meeting his wife he turned his life around and lived the second half as a respectable and peaceful man. It appears that she changed him. But I suspect the reality is that she gave him a reason to change himself. She's long since passed on now, but when I asked him about it, he said, "It finally boiled down to having a greater reason to stay sober than to raise Cain. That woman was good for my soul."

I think what women really mean when they say they want to change men is that they genuinely want to know how they can positively influence their man to help him be the best man he can possibly be. Perhaps I'm giving some women the benefit of the doubt, but let's proceed under the assumption that you have your husband's or boyfriend's best interests at heart. After all, you chose him like he is . . . you couldn't have possibly made that big of a mistake, could you?

While you may not be able to change a man, you certainly have the God-given ability to influence and motivate your man in ways that border on the miraculous. *In fact, your capacity to influence your man is one of the most potent forces on earth.* But to be truly effective you must understand how and why your influence works.

A woman can be like a trainer or a whisperer with a man. She can either try to bend him and change him to her will, or she can use her talents and skills to learn about him and help influence him through trust and love to be all he was meant to be.

Gary, a listener to Dr. Laura Schlessinger's program, made this comment: "A husband is like a horse. At the end of the day he is usually rode hard and put away sweaty. If his master drives and beats him, he'll go just so far before bucking and rebelling. [But] if you love him, if you coax him, he'll drive himself till his heart explodes before he will let his master down. He'll give himself to death for the one he loves. Which way should a woman handle a man?"[1]

When a man loves a woman, he will do almost anything she asks. Men have climbed mountains, swum oceans, and conquered armies all for the love of a woman. Delilah caused the downfall of the strongest man on earth, and Helen of Troy with her "face that launched a thousand ships" was the center of a ten-year war between nations.

Single women often lament that all the good men are already taken. Is this true? Maybe. But, just maybe all those men they admire who are taken are good, in part, because of the positive influence of their wives and girlfriends in their lives.

Women have an incredible influence in men's lives. The old saying "Behind every good man is a good woman" is not just hyperbole; it is the truth.

A Woman's Influence

> A man's wife has more power over him than the state has.
>
> Ralph Waldo Emerson

Can a woman "change" a man? Perhaps, but probably not in the sense some women may hope. And if you do succeed in "changing" him, it will probably have negative consequences. We've all seen the henpecked husband who does whatever his wife tells him to. He is an empty shell of a man. He's not happy and neither is she.

But a woman can use her powerful influence to subtly guide and lift a man up to be all he was created for. She holds the key to his success or failure as a man, husband, and father. This influence is delicate, understated, and nurturing as opposed to a male's bolder, more overt influence. It tantalizes a man with heady inspiration and inspires him to believe in himself that he possesses greatness. Her subtle, refined grace arouses within him a passion which emboldens his character and deeds.

The Percy Sledge song "When a Man Loves a Woman" talks about the extremes a man will go to for a woman's love—everything from turning his back on his best friend to sleeping out in the rain if his woman asks him.

That love he has for you gives you great power. Do you use that power for superficial gains or as a long-term investment in both your futures?

Most men won't change or grow on their own without some external motivation. But that love for you can motivate them to mighty changes. As Jack Nicholson says to Helen Hunt in the movie *As Good as It Gets*, "You make me want to be a better man."

In an equestrian competition called *dressage*, a skilled rider sits apparently motionless in the saddle as the horse performs an intricate series of movements, remaining relaxed, their performance appearing effortless. The goal of a horse and rider in dressage is to move as one—each knowing and anticipating the other's desires.

To some degree this is how a woman should approach her man—to encourage him to do something without anyone else seeing you do it. I don't believe that constitutes manipulating or controlling him. He wants to make you happy; he just doesn't know how. Your willingness to use your influence to gently steer him in the right direction makes both of you happy and more satisfied.

The Importance of Your Respect

Men today are confused about what their roles are and how best to live their lives. We get mixed messages from the media, the educational system, churches, and even the government. We don't know what's expected of us, and so we often hide rather than face rejection or failure. One thing that's been determined very clearly from workplace studies is that if employees don't know what is required, they cannot fulfill those expectations. They are also not very happy or satisfied with their situation.

A man's role used to be pretty clearly defined as a provider and protector of his family. While these roles are still fundamental, things have gotten much more complicated regarding relationships. Most women do not leave their husband because he is a poor provider; they leave because he does not fulfill her emotional needs.

I confess that I firmly believe women possess "women's intuition," but I also just as strongly believe that men do not. Your man really needs your help to understand your needs because he will not be able to meet them if he doesn't know what they are. Many women, consciously or unconsciously think, *Well, if he really loved me, he would know what my needs are.* Unfortunately, that is the way women think, not men. Sometimes, women are not even in touch with what they need; they just know they need something. It is unfair for you to expect him to be able to read your mind, or to understand your needs especially if you don't. *Your man has no mental framework to understand what your emotional needs are because he does not think the same way you do.*

I also believe that most men truly want to satisfy their women in all areas. They secretly yearn to reach their full potential and become worthy of admiration and respect from other men and especially their woman. A man garners his self-esteem from whether or not he can satisfy his woman. Your influence and whether or not he can satisfy your needs can make or break him as he goes through life.

Men want to understand women, but it seems like a monumental task. This reminds me of the story about the guy walking down a California beach. He looks down and sees a lamp sticking out of the sand. He picks it up, looks at it, and starts brushing the sand off from it. Suddenly in a puff of smoke, a genie appears! The genie says to the man, "I will grant any one wish you want."

The man exclaims, "Great! I've always wanted to go to Hawaii, but I'm scared to fly and I get seasick. Build me a bridge across the ocean so I can drive to Hawaii."

The genie says, "Do you have any idea how complicated and difficult that would be? The logistics alone make it impossible. It would cost billions of dollars. Isn't there anything else you'd like instead?"

The man says, "Well, I've always wanted to understand women."

The genie replies, "Do you want that bridge two lanes or four?"

While many men struggle understanding their wives, you are more important in his life than he may ever know. As a woman, you were designed by God to be your man's helpmate (Gen. 2:18), although the term "completer" might be a more accurate description of a woman's role with her man. A woman completes a man in ways he could never accomplish on his own. Of course any time God gives us this kind of responsibility, he also equips us to be able to perform it. Therefore, you have a unique opportunity to use this powerful influence that God gave you to help your man achieve his destiny. Make no mistake about it. God gave you a hugely powerful influence, which we will talk about throughout this book. But like any great power, you have to learn how to use it properly and respect the damage it can cause.

Power for Good

As a woman you can build a man up or tear him down merely by the level of respect you give to him and the amount of faith you have in him. Your tongue wields greater power than any double-edged sword.

I'm not sure if my wife began giving me respect and admiration before I started acting like a real man, or if the respect came after my actions. However, it's my perception that her offering respect and admiration (even if I didn't necessarily deserve it) was a major contributor to my changing from a complacent, self-centered man, husband, and father into an active, motivated man interested in lifting others up to help them reach their potential.

I do know that she taught me what love was. I grew up in an emotionally dangerous and often physically violent world.

I did not know how to love. My wife's patient example and teaching helped me to heal wounds that I didn't even know existed. Once I started to heal, I was more able and willing to fulfill her needs and desires. Without her nurturing nature and loving spirit, I do not know if I would have ever healed to the point of being able to truly enjoy life or love another person, much less myself. Needless to say, she has influenced my life tremendously. And because I influence many people through my work, she has contributed to the touching of many other lives as well. All because she used her feminine influence with her man the way God designed.

It takes much more work and effort to build something than it does to destroy it. Like either a skilled craftsman or a demolition contractor, a woman is capable of building up or tearing down her man. That's a big responsibility and a power that many women do not recognize. Some women, such as femme fatales, use their power for destruction and self-gain. Other women do not use it at all and become victimized. The best circumstance is where a woman understands her power and uses it responsibly to benefit her life and those of her entire family.

Many men have been brought to salvation because of their desire to be close to a cute young gal. And many a man, myself included, has gotten a new lease on life due to the love of a good woman.

A woman has incredible power. She can destroy her man with her words or she can help him become the man he could never be without her support, faith, and encouragement. There's not much a man can't deal with in life if he knows he can come home to a loving, supportive wife who respects him.

I made a couple of assumptions while writing this book. One is that the reader is already in a relationship with a man. Some of you may be still looking for a good man, but that is another book sitting on my desk just waiting to be published. The other assumption is that you are in a relationship with a reasonably good man. Maybe he isn't perfect, but at his core he's a good man with the potential to be better. You would like to know how best you can help him be the best man he can be. For those of you in relationships with bums, losers, abusers, addicts, or just plain bad men, you may need more help than this book can offer.

Much of this book is directed to help a woman understand how to fulfill a man's life and help him become more than he would be without her. A man also has a duty to help meet his woman's needs, but that too is another book.

This book will focus on how a woman can become indispensable to her man and will explore the ways a woman can use the incredible power God gave her to influence her man so that he becomes the kind of man he was created to be. We will look at everything you need to know (and some things you might not want to know) about your influence as a woman. We will examine what makes a good man and what character traits hold him back. We'll look at the power God gave you as a woman—both inspiring and destructive—and how it impacts a man's life. You'll learn the greatest strategies to empower him and the tactics most destructive to his soul.

When we are done, you will have the ability and insight to help shape, encourage, and inspire your man to greatness. You will hold in your hands the key to being . . . a Man Whisperer!

2

Authentic Masculinity

A man is created for challenges. He is equipped to overcome, to run the gauntlet, to stand firm as a well-anchored corner post. Men are the benchmark in life, society, and family. It is part of the masculine responsibility to demonstrate strength and stability, to protect and provide for those within their sphere of influence. This is the hallmark of manhood.

Preston Gillham, *Things Only Men Know*

Have you ever noticed both women and men are naturally drawn to certain men? People like being around this kind of man. You can't quite put your finger on what it is, but you know you like it. When he comes into a room or walks down the street, people automatically notice him—they see something different about him. It's not that he's particularly handsome or accomplished; there's just something invigorating and *attractive* about him. It's refreshing and feels *safe* to be around him.

You've just encountered authentic masculinity. It's rare, but it's out there. And it's the best thing you can encourage in your man.

How do you recognize healthy masculinity when you see it? It's rarely modeled on television, in newspapers, in music videos, or in movies. In fact, if you look at what the media often portrays, you've found just the opposite of healthy masculinity. We seldom see it modeled in politics, academia, the workplace, sports venues, or even in church. Much to our culture's shame, we seldom even see it held up as a virtue anymore.

How can a woman use her magnificent influence to help a man achieve his full potential if she doesn't know what his potential should look like? It's been my observation that some women are notoriously poor at recognizing authentic masculinity. So let's start by exploring how culture has negatively influenced masculinity, what healthy masculinity is, and most important, what role a woman plays in creating and encouraging authentic masculinity.

Cultural Influence

Our culture promotes behaviors in men that are unhealthy for marriages and families. Pornography is no longer a hidden, shameful activity; it is one of the fastest-growing sectors of our economy. Sexual promiscuity and adultery are no longer social taboos; they are winked at. Even so-called recreational alcohol and drug use is, if not encouraged, certainly tolerated. Addictions, whether chemical or sexual in nature, are "diseases" and not really anyone's fault. Our society does not even look askance upon abandoning your family if you're not happy anymore. The wreckage of these actions and attitudes is scattered across our cultural landscape in the form of broken families and broken hearts.

Even so, our culture continues to encourage our young people to engage in sexual experimentation and activity at younger and younger ages. As a result, primarily because males mature emotionally slower than females do, we have seen a dramatic rise in the number of teen fathers and young men abandoning their wives, girlfriends, and children. This promiscuous mentality has also resulted in an increase in grandparents raising their grandchildren.

The negative influence of the media on our young males is undeniable. Music videos glorify violence and sexual self-gratification. Movies and television programs often portray "heroes" who gratuitously kill and harm others and then enjoy casual, irresponsible sexual relations with a plethora of beautiful young women. Video games capitalize on the natural male attraction toward aggression, action-adventure, and competition to reinforce violent behaviors—the more graphic and violent, the better they sell. The media may not be the cause of male failure within our culture, but it certainly exploits their weaknesses for its own gain.

Only a few years ago one famous rap star was denounced for music lyrics that, among other things, promoted the killing of police officers. Today he is a spokesman for several large mainstream American companies. Star athletes are regularly indicted, arrested, tried, and convicted for crimes such as rape, sexual assault, battery, and even murder. Oftentimes within a few years these men are once again the darlings of the sports world with no apparent accountability for their actions. This tells young men in effect that being famous (or infamous) is more important than being a man of integrity. It also tells young women that men with these types of value systems are worthy of adoration.

Is it any wonder we are creating young men with a skewed perspective of what behaviors constitute healthy, authentic masculinity, and young women who can't spot a good man among all the posers?

What Is a Man?

What is a real man? What does he look like? How does he act? What characteristics separate him from an average guy? What factors can you use as a measuring stick to determine his authenticity?

Our culture generally tells us that, at best, the role of a man is to put his nose to the grindstone after finishing school and work hard the rest of his life. It tells us the mark of a man is how much money he makes and how many "toys" he acquires. His financial achievement determines his success in life. The American Dream is the standard by which we judge a man's success.

Men now are caught up in the self-centered, mundane pursuits of life. Most are apathetic and living lives filled with passivity—they lack decisiveness and commitment. They fail to see the higher purpose they were created for. Even the best of them often feel they are doing enough just by being a good guy, a caring person who does nice things for others occasionally—when it's convenient, that is. Most men are trapped in societal expectations and the search for self-gratification. We all (men and women alike) yearn for something meaningful, a cause to fight for—significance in our lives.

What men fail to realize is that freedom lies in following God's plan for their lives. Charles Colson says, "*Freedom lies not in conforming to the world's expectations or even realizing what we take to be our deepest wishes; it lies in following the call on our lives.*"[1]

An authentically masculine man puts aside his needs, desires, wants, and sometimes even his dreams for the benefit of others. He does this without fanfare and frequently without anyone even noticing. His life is not about *his* individual rights, achievements, or happiness; it's about making life better for others. His sacrifices are part of his character and give his life significance. He makes these sacrifices with the stoic nobility that God granted all men by right of their birth gender.

Too many boys grow up thinking that manhood means having the freedom not to do things you don't want to anymore, or doing only what you want. I see fatherless boys who grow up thinking that the world is about them and that women will serve and rescue them from every trouble and inconvenience they experience. But the reality is that being a man actually means being *required* to perform many things you don't want to do. It also means not doing many things you'd like to do.

A real man has honor. He stands tall as the fierce winds of adversity blow around him. He cherishes and protects women and children. He knows he has an obligation to mentor those who follow in his footsteps. He recognizes his sphere of influence and uses it for good. He understands that life does have fundamental truths and lives his life according to a firm set of principles. He uses his God-given warrior spirit to fight for justice and equality. He stands for *something*. Too many men today stand for nothing—they are directionless.

I am privileged to serve as a teacher and mentor for a dozen young men at a local Bible college who have agreed to spend time mentoring fatherless boys. I tell these young seminary students that they may never see the results or consequences of their actions during their lifetimes. But the work they are doing is eternal. They are helping to change the world. Every boy whose life they touch, and everyone whose life that boy touches, will be changed because of what these young men are doing today. I believe, as God looks at these students, he is beaming with pride. These young men are living lives of honor, and I am proud to be associated with them.

I have received many emails and letters from mothers of the boys these young men are mentoring. They each say, "The young men and the Standing Tall program have been an answer to my prayers." I tell my Mighty Men, "This is not just a figure of speech—these mothers mean this literally. They have been praying to God for help—many of them for years." *They are acting as God's agents in answering someone's prayers—someone who is hurting and desperate for help.* That is what men are created for—to help women and children; to seek justice, to encourage the oppressed, to defend the cause of the fatherless, and to plead the case of the widow (see Isa. 1:17). They are supposed to lift them up when no one else but God cares. They are here to help answer prayers. What a powerful call on their lives.

The sacrifice these young men are making for others' benefit with no expectations in return, despite carrying a heavy load of college credits and working part-time, is what authentic masculinity is all about.

A Life of Significance

> You are not here merely to make a living. You are here in order to enable the world to live more amply, with greater vision, with a finer spirit of hope and achievement. You are here to enrich the world, and you impoverish yourself if you forget the errand.
>
> President Woodrow Wilson

Men who exhibit authentic masculinity live lives of significance. They lift up others to help them achieve their potential. They make sacrifices in order to make a difference in the world—for everyone, not just their own family. They have passion and vision and are genuinely interested in giving of themselves for the betterment of others. And they probably don't make a big production out of doing it either. Men like this are other-centered, not self-centered. They are other-focused instead of self-focused.

These men do not just spend their time and energies on sating their own personal self-gratification. They put the welfare of their wives and children ahead of their own needs and wants. This kind of man wouldn't buy a fishing boat to indulge his own hobby if his wife needed braces for her teeth. He wouldn't go out bowling or drinking with the boys if his children needed help with homework. But he would take a temporary second job if his children needed something special that he didn't have the money for. He is financially responsible and has the proper perspective of work versus family.

These men recognize their obligations to their wives and children. If a father must work harder so the mother doesn't have to work outside the home, it is his duty to do so. Men who live lives of significance see the big picture. They have vision of a world bigger than their own hand in front of their face. Authentic men make good husbands and fathers because they know the true nobility that lies behind fulfilling their destiny as leaders in their homes and communities. Authentic men do not let evil flourish in the world by their inaction. They step forward and say or do something if they see an injustice taking place. Their very presence keeps much evil at bay. Just look at what happens to neighborhoods that have a high rate of fatherlessness, then compare them to neighborhoods with men actively involved with their families.

In the movie *Kingdom of Heaven*, a young widower blacksmith first meets his father as he travels to defend Jerusalem during the Crusades. His father introduces himself to his son for the first time and asks forgiveness for never having been a part of his life. With nothing to keep him in his village after the death of his wife and child, the young man follows his father and trains to become a knight. In the short period they are together before his father's death, the young man flourishes under his father's tutelage and follows in his footsteps, becoming a man of honor. Throughout the movie the young knight relies on his father's instruction and example. In one powerful scene near the end of the movie while he is preparing the city of Jerusalem against attack by overwhelming forces, he endows knighthood upon the city's commoners defending the city by quoting the same oath that his father did to him:

> Be without fear in the face of your enemies,
> Be brave and upright that God may love thee,
> Speak the truth even if it leads to your death,
> Safeguard the helpless.
> That is your oath![2]

The local high priest rebukes him by saying, "Who do you think you are? Can you alter the world? Does making a man a knight make him a better fighter?"

As the knight looks him in the eye and boldly proclaims, "Yes!" you can see all the men who have been charged with the challenge to greatness swell with pride and determination. They do in fact know that the expectations and exhortations of greatness can make a man more than he would be without the knowledge of God's vision for his and every man's life.

Authentic men are passionate, fierce, and noble—they care. In fact, they *are* dangerous, but it's a good dangerous. You might not see this passion on the exterior, but it's bubbling under pressure just beneath the surface, forcing its way into every area of his life. These men have a spiritual longing for adventure, for a battle to fight that's bigger than themselves, for significance in their lives. Those embers of passion may be banked down low in some men, just waiting for the right woman to come along and stoke those coals into a roaring flame.

When you see a man with a passion for something bigger and nobler than himself, you are looking authentic masculinity in the eye.

God's Representative

An authentic man is God's representative here on earth. He recognizes his responsibilities in God's eyes. He is the first example of the heavenly Father in his daughter's life, and he is the yardstick against which all other men are measured. Hopefully he is able to be an earthly example who reflects well on our heavenly Father and inspires others by his example. He is a role model of masculinity to his sons and daughters, and is the rock his wife depends upon. He is a giver of life.

Ernest Gordon describes what he learned about how men face life and death during his time in a Japanese prison camp during World War II: "Selfishness, hatred, envy, jealousy, greed, self-indulgence, laziness, and pride were all anti-life. Love, heroism, self-sacrifice, sympathy, mercy, integrity, and creative faith, on the other hand, were the essence of life, turning mere existence into living in its truest sense. These were the gifts of God to men."[3]

Gentleness, loyalty, forgiveness, dependability, kindness, courage, strength, wisdom, sacrifice, and patience are all godly, authentically masculine characteristics that some men display. Their example and leadership are what make the difference between the darkness of despair and the bright light of hope.

Spiritual Leadership

An authentic man is a spiritual leader in his home and the community. That may involve attending church regularly, saying grace before every meal, praying with his wife or girl-friend, and setting the example for those who follow him in all spiritual matters. It certainly involves consistently seeking a deeper relationship with God and being under his authority. If a younger man has been brought up with that kind of example, he is likely to be a spiritual leader in his own home as well. But if he hasn't been, a woman can influence him to pick up the spiritual leadership mantle.

Being a spiritual leader is particularly difficult for most men—likely because we feel inadequate to the task. When I first accepted Christ into my life at age forty, I was very reluctant to be a spiritual leader in my home. But with my wife's gentle encouragement (sometimes insistence), I slowly gained confidence. She respectfully followed my lead in spiritual matters even when I didn't have a clue what I was doing. This compelled me to seek out more knowledge in order to live up to her respect for me and her faith in me.

As he provides a spiritual role model, a man sets the expectations of his children in this area as well. One woman told me, "Because I have always known my dad as the spiritual head of the household and a man of God, I knew that's what I wanted in a husband . . . and now have."

A Woman's Responsibility

What role do women play in developing and maintaining men of honor within a culture? Is it about measuring the man only, or is it improving on her own inner yardstick she measures men by? Which comes first, the lowering of the standards in women by choosing lousy men, or lousy men being generated and encouraged by the lowering of the standards in women? Have women lowered their standards regarding men of character? Or are there simply fewer good men from which to choose?

As a collective gender, women have an awesome responsibility in the process of choosing and creating men of character. They do this not only by raising boys to become good men but by the character of the men they choose to have children with.

One of my friends suggested this section be titled "They can't all be jerks. Maybe it's you." Not very flattering, but it does speak to a significant issue—women have had the power throughout history to create the *type* of men a culture produces merely by their choice of those they mate with. It is a responsibility women don't often recognize. For instance, in the early years of civilization when hunting skills and physical strength were necessary to provide for and protect a family, only the strongest, fiercest, and dominant males were chosen by women to mate with.

As the Industrial Age dawned, our culture shifted from mere brute strength survival requirements, and other characteristics became more desirable to women—mechanical aptitude, employability, and dependability. Earning money to provide for luxuries over and above just basic survival became sought after.

The Information Age generated a desire for men with traits such as intelligence, wealth, material success, and stress assimilation. Today, as women have become more heavily involved in the economic marketplace and political arena, more feminized or gender androgynous traits such as gentleness, passivity, and indecisiveness (traits which in men often lead to apathy and lack of commitment) appear to be characteristics in men preferred by many women. At least that is the type of men many women are choosing or at least willing to have children with, which is ultimately what encourages certain types of behaviors in men.

Renowned author Don Miller states it much more practically in his discussion with college men:

> Women saying no to men, not letting men have sex with them, causes men to step up. If, in order to have sex with them, women demanded you got a job and shaved every day and didn't dress like a dork or sit around playing video games, then all of us would do just that. We all want to have

sex, right? . . . So if a woman demanded that you act like a gentleman . . . that you were able to commit and focus, then everybody in this room would do just that, if for no other reason than we want to have sex. And in turn this would be good for families, and would be good for communities. Let's face it, we're guys, and too often we are going to take the path of least resistance. Many of us are the way we are because women are attracted to a certain kind of man. We may not have realized this dynamic was shaping us, but it has been. Nobody is exempt. So, when sex is cheapened, we are getting what we want without having to pay for it. That's not good for anybody, not in the long run anyway.[4]

Regardless of the type of men she has been exposed to, a woman will need the faith to believe that God will provide the best man for her—a man with godly character (flawed but repentant). She will need to have more than a human desire to pick the right man who will be the father to their children, train them in the way they should go, and impart wisdom for their life.

Choosing, Not Settling

What woman, caught up in the hormonal whirlwind of falling in love, can be expected to be a prophetess, a seer—seeing more of the future than the present? There are, however, some skills or tips that can help a woman see into the future.

The best situation would be a woman who knows the Architect (God) who has drawn the blueprints of masculinity and relationships. She then knows how to read the blueprints, hires the contractor, supervises the work, and pays the bill. This woman knows the Lord, understands men by comparing them to those already in her life, takes the steps to seek out a potential husband without being overly attached, and is willing to pay the price of waiting—testing the structure as it progresses, and finally willing to pay the price for the long haul—for better or for worse, until death do us part.

Unfortunately (I've observed this many times in high school kids), there is a kindred spirit that seems to draw guys and girls together. There is something in one that attracts that something in the other. This drawing together isn't rational. Any onlooker would advise her to not marry this man, but the words fall on deaf ears. In her eyes, on this day, he is Mr. Right.

Single moms also fall into the trap of wanting someone even if it's just to help alleviate their burden. One woman I know, who has several children, is living with a man she is not married to. Because of her past choices of being involved with highly abusive men, she believes that this relationship is a step toward recovery and a healthy relationship. But two of the biggest responsibilities of an authentically masculine man are to provide for and protect his family. This man she lives with cannot provide for his new "family" because of his child-support responsibilities to the family he previously abandoned. Also, for whatever reason, she does not feel this new boyfriend can protect her or her children from their abusive father and so leaves town whenever the ex is rumored to appear.

Since her current live-in is fulfilling neither of his main priorities in their relationship, my question to her was, "Why are you with him?" Her response? "Because he is a nice guy." An admirable trait perhaps, but not a very good one to focus an entire relationship around. Really, the only purpose he serves is to keep her bed warm. Also, since he does not challenge her in any way to grow, he is not a threat to her sense of control. The example she is setting for her children is guaranteed to be emulated by them.

The danger is of selecting one's mate based on unknown standards. A woman needs to think about what kind of man she is willing to live with the rest of her life *before* she gives her heart away. She needs to consciously decide what character traits she wants and needs in a man ahead of time. Waiting to simply "fall in love with Mr. Right" often results in marrying Mr. Wrong. What woman would consciously decide to marry a philanderer, a drug addict, an alcoholic, or an abuser? Yet, many do. Not because that is what she really wants, but because emotion overrides her decision making.

One single mother I know has a history that appears to be somewhat typical of many women today. She is a bright, attractive woman (a former beauty pageant winner) whose first relationship was with a man who, for all intents and purposes, kidnapped her and held her captive in an abusive situation for several years until he nearly killed her and she escaped. Her second relationship was with a man who impregnated her and then abandoned her and her son. The last man she was involved with soaked her for every dime she had and then left her with massive debts and unpaid medical bills. While she is not responsible for these men's abusive behaviors, I cannot help but think she encourages that behavior by continuing to choose to sleep with men of low character.

I am not suggesting that the epidemic of fatherlessness our country currently faces is the fault of the women who have been abandoned by the men who impregnated them. That bane on our society is an indictment of men, not women. But I am saying that in some ways, women do bear at least a portion of the responsibility of rampant fatherlessness and low character in men purely by the choices they make. Men conform to the requirements and rules to which they are held accountable. This applies to relationships just as much as the business or sports world. *To put it bluntly, the character of the men* a woman sleeps with encourages that character in all men. If enough women sleep with men of low character, then men have no need to aspire to anything higher. If enough women reserve sex for marriage and choose only men of noble character, then that is what all men will aspire to be like. Either way, their offspring (male and female) will tend to follow in those footsteps modeled for them.

Some women I've spoken to resent that implied responsibility. But if women recognize their role as gatekeepers of authentic masculinity, men will hold authentic masculinity in high esteem again, instead of conforming to whatever lesser roles society offers to them. Protecting and promoting that role for men is in their own best interest in the long run, because that role of manhood eventually comes back to bless women's and children's lives.

Now that we know what authentic masculinity looks like, and how a woman influences it in a culture, let's look at some specific character traits in men that women can encourage and promote.

3

Nine Qualities of Good Men

The world is upheld by the veracity of good men: they make the earth wholesome. They who lived with them found life glad and nutritious. Life is sweet and tolerable only in our belief in such society.

Ralph Waldo Emerson, *Representative Men*

Horse whisperers are experts on horses. They understand what makes a horse tick. One of the most important things horse whisperers do before they attempt to interact with a horse is to learn about that horse's past and its history. Was the animal abused? What is its pedigree? What are its strengths and weaknesses? Why does it act the way it does? The whisperer then takes that knowledge along with his or her own experience to help communicate with the animal.

The whisperer also takes into consideration what breed the horse is and what specific traits and tendencies that breed exhibits. For example, is the horse an Arabian who is an extremely fast learner but easily bored? The Appaloosa is a hard worker with great stamina but needs lessons repeated many times before learning them. He's easygoing, curious, and inquisitive. He's also fearless but somewhat passive-aggressive. The quarter horse is a fast learner, and generally adaptable, patient, and compliant, whereas the Thoroughbred is known to be emotional, high strung, and overreactive.

The whisperer has a vision for what the horse can become. Whisperers have role models for what a healthy animal should look and act like. They don't just start trying to change a horse without an end vision in mind.

Likewise, it would be unwise to just start fiddling around trying to influence or improve your man without having some kind of idea what his temperament is like.

It is also important to know what a good man should look and act like. When I work with groups of men or women (especially those raised without good role models), I often find that they say they don't know what a good man looks like. In fact some women say they have never been exposed to or even *seen* a good man before. But when I survey them about what character traits a good man possesses, they nearly universally come up with the same ten or twelve character traits. They may not think they know what a good man looks like, but intuitively we all do. Let's explore what character traits a good man possesses.

Character Traits of a Good Man

Many men, especially young men, have not developed and matured into their full potential by the time they reach adulthood. Men of all ages also come in all levels of maturity: some men are grown up, some are in the process of growing up, and some will never grow up. They have a man's body, but mentally, emotionally, and psychologically they are still boys. A lot depends on a man's background, his character, and his willingness to grow. Men who do not grow up will steal a woman's youth, her security, and her happiness.

It takes seasoning, experience, spiritual growth, a good attitude, and the help of a good woman for a man to reach his full potential. However, he should already have at least several of the following character traits if you hope to help him develop his full potential as a man of character. If your man already scores high in these categories, take a moment to appreciate that you picked a good one.

Strong Work Ethic

Many, many women I've spoken with have been involved with men who either did not hold steady employment or else expected to be taken care of by the women in their lives. Men who have been raised by a mother who did everything for them are content to allow women to take care of them for the rest of their lives.

A man was meant to work—it's part of his makeup. Healthy men feel compelled to work—it's almost as if they can't help themselves. In fact, they have a burden to provide that always weighs upon their shoulders. Men who work but are unable to provide adequately are often very frustrated and angered by those circumstances. They may not always like their job, but they know working is one of their key roles in life and so they accept it. Men with a healthy masculinity enjoy accomplishing something by the sweat of their brow—it develops their self-esteem. It makes them feel like a man. It makes them feel powerful to be depended upon provisionally.

One of the most gratifying things I've ever accomplished was with my bare hands. I spent the better part of two summers disassembling, moving, and reassembling a huge aboveground/belowground swimming pool with a deck from the previous owner's home into our backyard. It must have had ten thousand screws, bolts, and nuts. It was hot, dirty, sweaty, frustrating work for a guy who is not an engineer, much less a plumber or an electrician. Now that it's finished, it isn't the prettiest swimming pool I've ever seen, but I'm darn proud of it.

What kept me going was my wife's encouragement. She would bring me a glass of ice water on those hot summer days. She would tell me how great it was coming along. She would cast a vision of what it would be like to have all the kids and their friends playing around the pool on summer days. She kept me going many times when I wanted to quit. And now she often tells me how grateful she is that I worked so hard so that she and the kids could enjoy the pool.

Men have been called by God to provide. Paul says, "But if anyone does not provide for his own, and especially those of his household, he has denied the faith and is worse than an unbeliever" (1 Tim. 5:8 NKJV). Because God created him this way, a man may feel like he is showering his wife with love by working long and hard. A woman can inadvertently sabotage his heart in this area by complaining. For instance, when she grouses and complains about how she doesn't feel like he loves her because he works so much, he is genuinely confused. The truth is, he is working hard precisely *because* he loves her so much.

Unfortunately men are not as important as providers today as they have been for thousands of years. Their primary role in life has changed, because now women are providers as well. That means most men do not get the satisfaction and appreciation they crave by working to provide for their families. In the past, men solved problems by working harder. Now when a man throws himself into his work, he compounds the problem by being away from his family, often exacerbating the problem.

Of course men, especially younger men, need to find a balance between work and family. It's easy for a man to get absorbed in his work because it's easier and safer for him than facing and managing the many aspects of a relationship. And young men get caught up in the desire to make their mark in the world. But understand that *providing for his family is one of the fundamental drives that God has placed within a healthy man.*

If you are married to a man who works hard and you are unhappy about it, recognize that there are many single moms out there who would give anything to be in your position, with a man who loves her enough to work hard to provide for her and their children. This issue, like many in life, is partly about your perspective.

One way to help a man put work into perspective is to help him understand that you are completely satisfied with the level of income he provides. Another is to help him understand how important his physical presence is to you and the children. If both of those fail, call him and tell him you've been thinking about him all day, the kids are at your mother's, and you can't wait until he gets home. If you do that a few times, he'll start looking forward to coming home.

An important thing to keep in mind is that if you allow the kids to constantly ask or expect material things beyond your means, then you're creating pressure on your husband to work longer hours. He will be less likely to scale back his work efforts if he thinks the needs of his family are not being met adequately.

Leadership Skills

A leader is a person you will follow to a place you wouldn't go by yourself.

Joel Barker

A man can lead a woman to places she wouldn't go by herself and never wanted to be. Or he can lead her to places she might not go on her own but finds a magnificent blessing because she does follow. The kind of leadership skills a man possesses helps to determine the life he leads and subsequently the quality of life of his family.

Not all men were created with bold, dynamic leadership skills, but all men were created to be leaders. Even a quiet, introverted man should at least be willing to make a decision and then be responsible for the consequences of that decision. Single men who avoid making tough decisions, or who are wishy-washy and waffle back and forth, will likely be reluctant to lead a family as well. Passivity and apathy are rampant diseases of the male gender. They apparently always have been, as evidenced by Adam's willingness to stand by and watch Eve disobey God's directive. Those inherent flaws have been encouraged by our culture until men are now *expected* to be self-centered and self-focused. These character deficits also lead to lack of commitment in men.

One Woman's Description of a Good Man

- He has a solid accountability network with peers and a mentor.
- He has a clear set of values that guide his behavior and decisions.
- He is authentically interested in what is best for you.
- He is supportive of your goals and dreams.
- He is sacrificial in giving to others.
- He has control over his sexual desires.
- He has freedom to share his emotions in a healthy manner.

A woman can encourage her man by telling him she respects him, that she's proud of him, and that she appreciates his efforts, especially when he steps out of his comfort zone and shows good leadership traits. More than anything, a man wants to feel respected and admired by his wife (or any woman in his life). When you use those messages to motivate (not manipulate) him, he will be eager to get that kind of feedback from you again.

Sometimes a woman has to push her man to take the leadership reins—especially spiritually. My wife had to nearly pull me along dragging and kicking to assume spiritual leadership for our family.

A man's actions always speak louder than his words. With that in mind, leadership by example is one of the best ways of leading a family. People usually heed what you do, not what you say.

Leaders inspire others through their encouragement, vision, and passion. They help others to be successful. The greatest leaders are people who put the best interests of others ahead of their own.

A man with leadership ability is accountable to others. If a man is accountable only to himself, he eventually does things that seem right but lead to destruction (for himself and others). The things he does might even be for the right reasons. But without someone to whom he is accountable, he will make decisions that are costly. When a man is accountable to no one except himself, he does not feel there is any reason to refrain from engaging in destructive activities such as visiting topless bars, viewing pornography, abusing drugs or alcohol, and succumbing to promiscuity, lying, stealing, cheating, and any or all other vices a man engages in.

"There is a way that seems right to a man, but in the end it leads to death" (Prov. 14:12). Never underestimate a man's potential for depravity when he is accountable only to himself.

Vision

A man needs a long-term vision for life. His vision should include looking out for those closest to him. I've told several of the young men who have dated my daughter that, while it's great that they are willing to protect her physically if necessary, it's better to have the foresight to make sure they do not put her in a situation where she *has* to be protected in the first place. That's having manly vision.

Part of having vision is the ability to plan ahead. A man should have a responsible plan on how to approach life. Men with vision are able to take a long-term approach to dealing with finances instead of satisfying their urges for instant gratification. A man should have a plan to provide the things that his wife and children will need in the future—a college education, a home, retirement planning, insurance needs, and a dependable budget. He doesn't allow his family to be at the mercy of whichever way the winds of life blow them.

Sometimes this means making decisions that are unpopular with his wife and children. But knowing what's best for them in the long term, he sticks to his guns under the pressure of popular opinion.

That's not to say that a man does not include and take into consideration his wife's opinions, desires, and wisdom, but he still needs to have the vision of seeing the big picture and using principles to base his decisions upon. He also recognizes that he is responsible and accountable for the decisions he makes. Many women tend to be more focused on the here-and-now needs of their family and so struggle with a long-term view of life. That's an important trait when you are the most crucial nurturer of a family unit. But that's why it's even more important for a man to provide this much-needed element to a relationship.

Many men, especially those raised in the world of women, are taught to make decisions using feelings instead of principles. But a man must use principles to make important decisions in life. For instance, there have been many situations where I did not *feel* like letting my children suffer the consequences of their choices and actions, but it was the right thing to do in the long run. In fact the decisions I regret most in life are those I made ruled by emotion and not principle.

A man with a servant-hearted leadership style will always seek to do what is best in the long run for those he loves. He doesn't settle for short-term gains. He won't be swayed by what's popular or because someone gets upset as a result of his best decision.

You can encourage your man by reminding him of his natural bent in this area. Encourage him that men are often better at long-term vision and that you need him to provide that skill for the family. Many men do not intentionally misuse or waste their gifts; we just forget sometimes. Your gentle reminder and encouragement helps keep us on track with the roles we need to fulfill within a family and in a relationship.

Honesty and Integrity

Integrity is doing the right thing for the right reasons no matter the circumstances. Integrity is not situational ethics. A man with integrity values what is right over what is popular. That provides a foundation upon which to build integrity and leadership skills.

Men with integrity are honest. The dictionary defines *honest* as free from deception, truthful, genuine, real, reputable, credible, marked by integrity, frank, upright, just, conscientious, honorable. Are there any character traits listed here that you don't want the man in your life to be known for? Frankly, I'd rather be known as a man of integrity over a man with a lot of money any day. *The character of the man in your life reflects upon your reputation by association.*

Part of having integrity is being dependable—people knowing they can count on us. A man's word should be his bond. In fact, a man's word is the measure of his character. If he gives his word to someone, he is making a covenant with them. So, for instance, if he tells his wife and children that he loves them, then turns around and verbally abuses them, breaks his promises, or acts irresponsibly, he has not lived up to his word. You cannot love someone and simultaneously lie to them or mistreat them. It is incongruous behavior. Honesty and integrity keep men from making those kinds of mistakes in their lives.

One National Football League pregame show asks players whether they would rather be known as "nice" or "honest." I'm always surprised at how many of these star-athlete "men's men" respond with "nice."

A man of integrity speaks the truth with love rather than worrying about being nice.

Respect

Public address announcers at sporting events now have to remind men to remove their hats during the singing of the National Anthem. Teenage boys feel it is their "right" to play car stereos loud enough to rattle windows in houses blocks away. People drive around while talking on cell phones, eating, shaving, and applying makeup, and then deny culpability when they cause an accident. Young people walk three abreast along the sidewalk and refuse to step aside for their elders.

Many of the most influential paradigms (the music and entertainment industries most notably) of our selfish culture encourage lack of respect for authority. Newspapers continually berate police officers for overstepping their supposed boundaries, often siding with the lawbreakers.

Because receiving respect is so important to a man's self-esteem, the whole concept of respect is intrinsic to their being. Young men in gangs are willing to kill each other over the issues of respect and disrespect. Conversely, boys who have been trained in the concept of respect have a healthy understanding of the correlation between being respectful to others and receiving respect in return.

It's been said that how a man's father treated his family is a good indicator of how he will treat his own wife and children.

I don't know if that is true in every case or not, but I do know that a father's influence on his son is monumental. If a man's father is a man who respected others and was a healthy leader of his family, it's a pretty good bet that his son will share those values and characteristics.

Look for certain characteristics that will indicate what level of respect a man has for others. How does he treat his mother and other members of his family? Does he look up to his father or does he disregard his advice and wishes? How does he treat your mother and father? What is his attitude toward those people who are of no direct value to him? How does he treat animals? What about disabled individuals? What is his attitude toward his boss and co-workers? Does he fear and respect God? More than just how he acts, what is his internal attitude? Is he contemptuous or envious of others? How does he treat women? Does he accord them the same respect that he would want his mother or sister treated with?

The manners a man exhibits also speak volumes about his character and level of respect for others. A man who spits and belches all the time would not appear to have much respect for others. I used to work with construction workers. They would often plug one nostril and blow their noses onto the ground without a tissue. That behavior is pretty disgusting even just among men. I hear from my teenage daughter of many young men in high school who are not ashamed to loudly pass gas during class. Even though that makes me smile as I write it (I am still a man, after all), it doesn't seem very respectful of the young women around them.

The amount of respect a man shows toward others is the level you can expect to receive from him after you're married. A man who respects himself will treat others with respect.

He's more than likely the kind of man who can honor and cherish a good woman.

You can help him respect himself by showing him he is worthy of respect. Point out when others show him respect even in small ways. Discuss areas where he is gifted that he could use to receive respect from others. Let him know how important it makes others feel by his gift of respect to them. Most of all, respect yourself, so that he respects you; otherwise your input will not mean anything to him. For instance, if you allow him to speak or act disrespectfully to you with no consequences, he will consider your advice unworthy of attention.

Perseverance

Being in an intimate relationship is hard work. Anyone who is married will testify to that fact. Raising a family is hard work. I can tell you that some of the challenges my wife and I have encountered while raising teenagers have been some of the most difficult and stressful situations in my entire life. Working to support a family is hard and often frustrating.

Men who have been consistently rescued by their mothers instead of being held accountable for their choices and actions learn to rely on women to take care of them. If a man has learned early in life to quit when the going gets tough, it easily becomes a habit and he is likely to quit when really difficult struggles occur later on. Unfortunately when a man quits on his family and marriage, he devastates other people's lives, not just his own.

A man who quits every time a duty becomes difficult or who avoids challenges, only taking on tasks that he knows he can succeed at, will likely lack perseverance during the tough struggles of life. Watch your man to see how he perseveres in the face of adversity. Does he meet challenges head-on, or does he avoid unpleasant situations like the plague? Is he invigorated by the challenges of life, or does he stick his head in the sand until they pass?

A man who believes in himself will not have a fear of failure, avoiding circumstances and situations he does not feel he can deal with. That man will have the intestinal fortitude to stick it out through the tough times of marriage and raising children. It doesn't matter if he succeeds every time or not; what counts is that he tried and did not quit. Remember, adversity does not necessarily build character in a man—but it does reveal it.

Encourage your man daily. You cannot imagine how difficult it is to be a man in today's environment. He is bombarded daily with negative messages and few words of encouragement. Let him know the rewards that come from not quitting when the going gets tough. When you believe in him, he believes in himself. Your faith gives him courage, and it takes courage and bravery to be a man who matters today. There's not much a man can't persevere through with a good woman standing by his side.

Loyalty

How does one develop loyalty in a man? You teach loyalty by being loyal. Those who follow a loyal man know that he always has their best interests at heart. They know he will stand by them even when everyone else is against them. Loyal husbands and fathers tend to produce loyal families.

Loyal people stick with you when all else is in turmoil. Loyal people will still love you, even when they know you. They are people who, despite your human failures, still believe in you. They are friends and family members who will defend you to others even at the risk of their own popularity. Do you boldly defend your husband when you hear others—even your mother—criticize him? That is not the same as making excuses for him—it is proudly proclaiming your loyalty.

When your husband is convinced that you are loyal to him, that everything you do is for his best interests, he will be loyal to you. Loyalty begets loyalty.

Self-Discipline

An authentically masculine man has the self-discipline to succeed in life. Remember that, for purposes of this book, we are not defining success by our culture's definition of manly "success"; we are defining it by the standard of "authentic masculinity." However, I've found that most men who are authentically masculine also succeed in life according to our culture's definition. It seems to be a blessing or by-product of their faithfulness.

Most men reach a certain stage in life and then just stop growing and developing. They get a job, a family, and a few responsibilities that require much of their time and energies, so they focus on one or all of those areas. They seem to be content to settle for their lot in life. Then they wake up at fifty or sixty years old and wonder what has become of their lives. In a panic they try to relive their youth by driving expensive cars or having affairs with younger women. Never having attempted to live lives of significance, they now find themselves scrambling to leave a legacy, any legacy, to be remembered by.

Men with self-discipline use their time efficiently in order to pursue ventures that will help them grow and lift up others. For instance, instead of wasting all his spare time watching professional wrestling on television or drinking and carousing with the "boys," a disciplined man is more apt to prepare himself to grow in order to meet the needs of his wife and children. His hobbies are probably constructive instead of destructive.

Because I was not in a position to be able to afford to attend college right out of high school, I joined the military in order to get at least a portion of my schooling paid for. I then worked full-time and attended school at night over a period of many years in order to obtain my college degree. Frankly, I would have rather been doing any number of other things during those years instead of going to school and doing homework in my spare time. Also, because I was shy and somewhat socially inept, I knew I needed to develop speaking skills. Despite my strong aversion to public speaking, I joined Toastmasters International, attending meetings in the early mornings before work started. Fortunately I was blessed with a love for reading, so over the ensuing years I not only read for fun but also read nearly every personal-growth book I could lay my hands on. I've spent the past five years not only running a business but developing and directing a speaking ministry and writing books in my spare time. I did these things to better myself, and they required every ounce of self-discipline I could muster.

I tell my son and daughter that you can tell a lot about a man by looking at his house and car. A man with self-discipline keeps up with the maintenance on his house and automobiles. He considers these things investments, not just disposable assets.

Instead of watching movies filled with gratuitous sex and violence, he enjoys movies with positive male protagonists. Men are hardwired to be drawn to movies with action and adventure, so most of these will have some level of violence. One way to differentiate between what might be considered acceptable violence versus unacceptable is to consider the source or purpose. For instance, gratuitous violence for the sake of shock value, such as in a movie like *Pulp Fiction*, is damaging to a man's psyche. However, violence in pursuit of a noble cause, as seen in a movie like *Rob Roy* or *Braveheart*, is inspiring to a man's character.

After we finished watching the movie *Batman Begins*, I commented to my wife that it contained everything needed to be a successful "guy" movie—a noble cause worth fighting for, a damsel in distress who needs rescuing from an evil villain, a cool car and car chases, fighting, action, explosions, great gadgets, and good triumphing over evil. It was the kind of adventure that every man secretly yearns for in his life.

I believe the single most important factor that separates men who fail and those who succeed in life is reading. The types and quantity of books, magazines, and journals a man reads and feeds his mind with determine how far he goes in life. Because many men are poor readers, this effort requires huge reserves of self-discipline. Frankly, our culture and the educational system do a poor job of encouraging males to become readers.

A man who grows has the self-discipline to continue learning even after he finishes school. He continues to learn and educate himself. This can be accomplished by reading a variety of books, attending classes and workshops on a variety of topics, meeting with other men, or even being involved in healthy hobbies and activities. A healthy man works on growing all four of the intrinsic facets of his character: his physical health, his spiritual being, his mind (education), and his relationships.

These men also have the discipline to understand that "all work and no play makes Jack a dull boy." They enjoy recreational time with family and friends in healthy environments and pursuits. Healthy pursuits might be any outdoor activities, participation in sports, hunting, fishing, working on automobiles, playing music, painting, or a host of other creative and productive diversions. Unhealthy hobbies might include drinking or drug use, gambling, or any of a hundred other nonproductive activities.

Help a man build self-discipline by subtly directing and encouraging disciplined behavior. For instance, if your husband needs a little help in the weight or fitness categories, you can encourage him by joining him in healthy activities. Keeping healthy snack foods around so he's not tempted by poor choices, joining him at the gym, and taking evening walks with him all encourage him to make healthy choices.

Honor

Because there is very little honor left in American life, there is a certain built-in tendency to destroy masculinity in American men.

Norman Mailer, *Cannibals and Christians*

Honor is the heart of authentic masculinity. Throughout history men of all races and origins have sought to live lives of honor. Only recently has masculine honor been swept under the rug of moral relativism.

The French call it *noblesse oblige*—the obligation of honorable, generous, and responsible behavior associated with high rank or birth. In England, knights were taught to excel in the arms, to show courage, to be gallant and loyal, and to swear off cowardice and baseness. The Japanese had a warrior class known as *samurai*. These warriors lived by Bushido, a life of honor. Samurai had no fear of death. They would enter any battle no matter the odds. To die in battle would only bring honor to one's family and one's lord.

Men need honor. It is essential to our being. Men are programmed for performance, so they are very conscious of how they perform.

Being honorable and having the ability to give honor is an important factor in becoming an effective husband and father. Honor often requires us to put others' needs ahead of our own. Men without honor become undisciplined and dangerous in their relationships. Without a clear sense of honor, they have no foundation to stand on, and become overwhelmed by the needs of others.

Like most things, the best way a woman can encourage honor in her man is by being honorable herself, to commend him whenever she sees it in him, and to admire it in other circumstances and situations.

If you want to marry a man with the character traits we discussed in this chapter, you need to have your radar up so you can be aware of men who exhibit them. This requires a woman to be intentional in selecting the kind of men she dates and enters into relationships with. Some women who've grown up with a positive role model just naturally migrate toward good men. But if you are one of the many who have not, please be cognizant of the type and character of the men you are attracted to and the reasons why. Your choice in this area can lead to a life spent in bliss or one of misery.

If you are married, take a moment to consider these masculine traits. I suspect you'll find your husband has several of them. He is, in fact, one of those good men, and he needs you to recognize and affirm his good qualities. Sometimes we get so close to a person we forget to appreciate their true value in our lives.

4

Nine Traits That Hold Him Back

> Some women want a passive man if they want one at all;
> the church wants a tamed man—they are called priests; the
> university wants a domesticated man—they call it tenure-
> track people; the corporation wants a . . . sanitized, hairless,
> shallow man.
>
> Robert Bly, *Iron John*

A woman shouldn't fool herself into thinking she has the capability to change a man's core character. You cannot "fix" a broken man, no matter how much you want to. You can't lift up a character-flawed man; he will only pull you down. A woman cannot change a man's essential character—only God can do that. But she can enhance or diminish whatever qualities a man already possesses.

A man's core character includes values that were established during childhood. Some wounds (if known) can be soothed or even healed with a woman's influence, but much of the character he developed through example, modeling, and his childhood environment is deeply established. While not all men who were exposed to poor role models grow up to follow in those footsteps, many do. Many women have thought they saw something in a man that was not there. They thought they could nurture his good side or bring out his "real" character. Most of these women have suffered for their good intentions.

From my observations, I believe women are more willing to grow and change on their own. Especially as it pertains to relationships, women are always more willing to seek out knowledge to solve whatever problems exist. This is a generalization, of course, but it is women who attend most of our seminars and purchase the vast majority of our resources.

Men seem to need some sort of exterior motivation in order to be willing to change. Either they have to be miserable, on the verge of losing their wife and children, or mired in pain before they willingly seek help. They almost have to be tricked into attending seminars or workshops that address relationship issues. This may be in part due to their "fix yourself" mentality, or perhaps it's the fear of change we all possess.

Predictive Behaviors

One thing that is very helpful in all relationships is looking for predictive behaviors. Employers often ask potential employees questions about how they have acted in certain situations in the past. The way a man acted in the past probably indicates how he will act in the future.

For instance, if he's been married and divorced several times, the likelihood is that he will divorce again. If he has been violent or abusive in the past, he's probably going to be again. Has he fathered children with multiple women and abandoned them all? Does he quit or get fired from jobs all the time? Has he been promiscuous? You get the point.

Certainly, the redemptive grace of God can and does change men all the time, but short of that, people don't change dramatically all that often.

It's also important to remember that whatever character flaws we each have are magnified under pressure. When we are dating someone, we always put our best foot forward in order to impress the other partner. Only after we have captured our "prize" do we relax and let our true colors show. During the stress of marriage and raising a family, we are put in a pressure cooker environment. The character flaws that we have been able to conceal during the courtship process are then exposed, oftentimes too late.

Rest assured that life will test us severely and no one will be exempt. When challenges come, you want a man who has the character to endure the struggles and grow from the experience.

Perfect men don't exist, so your man will never be "perfect." However, the following character issues and behaviors are danger signals, like the flashing lights and bars at a railroad crossing. Remember that we are speaking in generalities here. All men will exhibit some of these characteristics to varying degrees, and many men will learn to control or change these behaviors as they grow and mature.

Some of the traits below may require professional counseling to resolve. However, if a woman is aware of these traits and the problems connected to them, she can be much more proactive rather than reactive in her approach to dealing with them.

Attitude

One of the best indicators of a man's character is his attitude. You can learn much about a man just by observing his posture and the way he interacts with others. Is he quick to anger when he believes he has been slighted? Does he laugh when someone gets hurt or insulted? Is he delighted when the plans of others fail? Does he frown much of the time? Does he boast and use foul language? Does he distrust authority?[1]

These are signals that he does not have an attitude that respects and honors others. If his attitude is like that toward others, it will eventually be that way toward you as well. It's the difference between a boy and a man.

Another example is that boys tend to spit and swear in public, but men shouldn't. It's disrespectful of others. There are other activities and functions that men don't perform in public as well.

I started introducing my son, Frank, to the wilderness when he was very small. We began taking hikes and camping from a very early age. When Frank was about three years old, the next-door neighbor lady briskly walked over and told me about an incident that had happened earlier in the day. It seems Frank was over playing with her children in their backyard when he called a time-out. He then calmly walked over to the nearby bushes, pulled his pants down, and proceeded to "whiz" on the bushes right in front of everyone. Flustered, the lady nervously laughed, "Frank, what are you doing?" Frank calmly explained, "I'm going to the bathroom."

She said, "But that's not something we do outdoors."

Frank then matter-of-factly replied, "Why not? My dad does it all the time."

You can imagine my embarrassment as she skeptically looked at me with a raised eyebrow while I tried to explain. "Well, uh, you see, uh, we go hiking, uh, in the woods, you know. He must have misunderstood about, uh, you know, where it's appropriate to, uh . . ."

Things just seemed to deteriorate from there as I tried to explain to her that I do not, in fact, go to the bathroom in our backyard.

The moral of this story is, boys urinate in public—men don't.

A man's appearance and how he takes care of his things can tell you a lot about his character as well. If he's disheveled with poor personal hygiene, multiple body piercings or tattoos, and a nonchalant attitude about being on time, it might indicate a lack of respect for himself and for others. I always figured that a man who wouldn't make the effort to clean up his car before a date did not have much respect for the girl. And I'll admit I'm a little old school and probably out-of-date on fashion trends, but I've always been a little suspicious of a guy who doesn't wear socks or underwear as well.

Many times men with bad attitudes are men who have been hurt. There is the old saying that "wounded people wound other people." A woman's influence in using her natural nurturing skills to help him overcome these wounds can help him to eventually be more compassionate toward others. Since we can't really love others until we love ourselves, part of a woman's influence is to help a man understand how worthy of love he is.

Anger

Anger in a man often masks some form of insecurity. Anger is a secondary emotion that many men use to cover other emotions that are less comfortable for them. For instance, a man might exhibit anger when he is feeling scared, vulnerable, or insecure. He may also resort to anger when he is physically injured or even tired. These other emotions, like fear, are more humiliating emotions for a man to experience than anger. Anger is a much more manly and comfortable emotion for a man. It's also easy for a man to get into the habit of using anger to mask other emotions. Sometimes it takes hard work to sort out what he is really feeling and its root causes. It's an effort that some men would rather not pursue when anger is so easily available.

Healthy anger in a man should not be repressed. For example, anger over injustice can be a healthy tool for a man to use. But unhealthy anger can manifest itself in behaviors such as belittling others, mean-spiritedness, taunting, criticizing, abuse, pettiness, or looking down on others. Condescension, dissatisfaction, complaining, passivity, envy, and uncooperativeness are also behaviors often caused by buried anger or resentment.

Men who exhibit passive-aggressive tendencies often have buried anger within themselves. Rather than confront the source of their anger, they hide it and manifest it by making others miserable. The term *passive-aggressive* is used to describe someone who exhibits manipulative behavior within their personality. On the surface, the traits may appear as stubbornness or a polite unwillingness to agree with a situation. The end result is that the person is really manipulating *you* to turn to their way of thinking. It can manifest itself as resentment, stubbornness, procrastination, sullenness, or intentional failure at doing requested tasks. One example of a passive-aggressive person would be someone who takes so long to get ready for a party they do not wish to attend that the party is nearly over by the time they arrive.[2]

Men who are angry a lot of the time generally have unresolved issues that they have not worked through—issues that the pressures of supporting and nurturing a wife and children are more likely to compound than help resolve.

Remember also that men who were raised without a father or a positive male role model are often angry. They are angry because they are scared. They are scared because a man never showed them how a man is supposed to act, make decisions, solve problems, and live his life. A man never modeled for them a healthy way to love a woman or raise children. The world is a difficult place to function in when you don't know the rules. It is very scary for a young man to be on his own when he doesn't know what to do or what is expected of him. Instead of being afraid (and thus humiliated), he instinctively turns to his old friend anger for comfort and solace.

Many times in order to uncover the issues that trigger anger, professional counseling is needed before healing can begin. However, there are several very effective anger resolution programs being facilitated through various churches. These programs can be very beneficial in helping a man understand and resolve these issues. Additionally, the presence of other healthy, authentic men in his life who provide counsel and accountability can serve to help a man with anger issues.

False Self-Esteem

We've all seen young men posturing, strutting around cocksure, acting the "playa," or "pimpin.'" The music-video rap culture encourages treating females as sexual playthings. This culture produces a subtle brainwashing effect that encourages boys to treat women poorly, and girls to expect to be treated strictly as objects of desire. I'm genuinely confused that the feminist movement isn't using their powerful political influence to combat this cultural asphyxiation of young women's psyches.

Males with a true, positive self-esteem do not need to buy into this posturing attitude. They recognize that treating women with honor and respect is more manly than subjugating them to sexual bondage and use for their own self-gratification. It's the difference between leadership that lifts others up versus one that holds others in bondage.

Males develop a positive self-image from significant accomplishments and by overcoming difficult circumstances under the guidance of positive male role models. A male who has never been held accountable to anyone or who hasn't been raised with boundaries where he can safely grow into manhood is likely to feel inadequate about his masculinity and overcompensate through exaggerated caricatural masculine behaviors.

What might seem like a high level of self-esteem on the outside is really a feeling of frightened inadequacy on the inside. Women can use their influence by not buying into our culture's version of masculine and feminine roles and behaviors. They can insist on being treated with respect and dignity by all males.

Poor Self-Confidence

> A hesitant man is the last thing in the world a woman needs. She needs a lover and a warrior, not a Really Nice Guy.
>
> John Eldredge, *Wild at Heart*

Poor or low self-confidence is different from low self-esteem in that a man can feel good about himself as a man and still lack confidence in one or more areas of his life. Unfortunately, this lack of confidence can spill over into all other areas of his life.

Lack of confidence within a man is one area where a woman can really make a big difference. Men who struggle with a lack of confidence are always second-guessing themselves. They are usually afraid to take risks or try anything new. Oftentimes the frustration of not feeling competent causes them to be angry or lose control of themselves. It can cause them to be discouraged and unsure. A lack of confidence in a man contaminates all areas of his life—from his work to his family. It chokes the life out of his passion. Many men who are uninvolved fathers or distanced husbands are often just ones who lack confidence in their abilities. Men tend to shy away from things in which they think they will not succeed. A man who is concerned that he will fail as a husband and father might tend to disappear rather than face potential failure.

When a man lacks confidence about something, he is typically fearful to try it. Hence, he enters into a vicious cycle of the lack of confidence leading to avoidance, avoidance leading to lack of self-confidence, and so on and so forth.

Lack of self-confidence keeps men from achieving their full potential in life. It causes them to settle for a mundane and nonthreatening lifestyle that can eventually lead to boredom and discontent. A man with poor self-confidence will not attempt to better himself, even for the benefit of his family. He is afraid to take risks for fear of failing.

But here is the miraculous, persuasive power of a woman—when his woman believes in him, a man automatically starts to believe in himself. His self-confidence rises and he becomes more willing to risk failure or success. And as his self-confidence rises, his anger diminishes. With true self-confidence comes positive self-esteem, and the need for displays of false masculine prowess disappears. The love, confidence, faith, and belief a woman has in a man can heal his wounds and cast out many of the demons that trouble his soul.

I've seen it on the basketball court many times. A player will not have any confidence in his abilities, and no matter what I do or say, he will continue to doubt himself. But let a little gal come along and whisper in his ear and suddenly he's Michael Jordan. His whole demeanor changes and he becomes the most self-assured, confident player on the team.

Self-Centeredness

When a man is self-centered, he puts himself and his needs before all others', including his wife's and children's. Young men tend to naturally be a little selfish and self-involved. But a man who continually looks out for number one in all of his relationships is a man who will probably always struggle with thinking of anyone besides himself.

Some men never grow up. They never develop the self-discipline needed to grow from a boy into a man. So many areas of a man's life require self-discipline. Yet so many men are being raised without it. This causes them to grow into men who focus exclusively on their own needs and wants.

Men with doting or dominant mothers typically become self-centered and self-indulgent. They want the comfort and security provided by Mom, plus the added benefits of sex. A pretty great combination! Unfortunately there are plenty of needy girls out there who will provide this for them.[3]

The trap in this scenario is that a self-centered man puts his needs ahead of a woman's until eventually she doesn't know who she is as an individual. She ends up believing her needs are not important. Because women are nurturers, it is sometimes difficult for them to see this character flaw in a man until it's too late. Like a Venus flytrap, a man can bait a woman by making her feel needed and then ambush her by gradually luring her into the sticky part of the snare to die.

Self-centeredness comes from immaturity. A woman can use her influence to help a man mature by helping (maybe forcing) him to recognize and suffer the consequences of his decisions. If you bail him out or rescue him every time he makes a poor decision, he will never mature. If you continually sacrifice your needs for his, he will never grow. Unfortunately, if his mother and father never taught him a man's responsibility of focusing on others' needs, you may have to.

Feminized Men

Many young men in our society, having been raised only by female authority figures, have been feminized. They have only seen female responses to life's challenges modeled. This is not to say that they are effeminate. Feminized men can look manly on the outside, but they have inner qualities more associated with femininity. These men are often passive and indecisive in their lives and relationships. Having had only females to guide them to manhood, they do not know masculine responses to problem solving and living life. Having lacked the role models to develop masculine leadership skills, they tend to either shy away from challenges and problems or look for a woman to take care of them. They go from a doting mother to the doting care of a girlfriend, and if that doesn't work out, they return to their doting mother.

The past several years I've spent a good amount of time waiting for flights in airports. I love to people watch. Lately I've noticed how many young women are with passive young men. These well-put-together and competent young women are often with frail-looking, passive young men who acquiesce to every one of their wishes. These young men appear to be nice young fellows but look "soft" and even somewhat timid. They appear to have no vitality or passion about them. They do what they are told and allow the young lady to make all the arrangements, to dictate their schedule and agenda. (By not being in a leadership role, they never risk being criticized or making a mistake.) Nearly to a couple, when they get up to board the plane, the young man dutifully picks up the smaller bags, and leaves the young woman to haul the larger, heavier bags (perhaps a form of passive-aggressive reprisal). The young woman seems to resignedly accept this burden as part of her leadership responsibility.

These young men don't look as if they could physically protect a woman if necessary. They look as if they could be blown over by a strong wind. At least once in every relationship a time will come when a man has to protect or defend a woman's honor. It would be an interesting experiment to walk up and start openly flirting with her in front of him to see how he would react. I wonder if these young guys will have the steel and gritty leadership necessary to weather the violent storms of marriage and raising a family.

Feminized men often marry strong, competent women who believe them to be sensitive and fair-minded men. But the woman quickly becomes frustrated by his lack of leadership. The more frustrated she gets, the more passive and indecisive he becomes. Eventually she loses respect for him, often signaling the end of their relationship.

Or these feminized men might react just the opposite, becoming angry, domineering, and abusive. They become hostile to females and feminine authority. They are often physically abusive and have children with multiple partners, abandoning all of them.

By putting a man into a leadership role, a woman's influence can eventually inspire him to become less passive over time. My wife was very good about insisting that I take a leadership role in many areas of our family, even when I was reluctant. Of course when she insisted that I take the lead, she had to resist the temptation to criticize my decisions even if I didn't do things the way she thought they should be done.

A man who is hostile toward women may well need more help than a woman's influence alone can provide. He may need professional counseling.

Jealousy

It is a greater compliment to be trusted than to be loved.

George MacDonald

Not trusting a man is a pretty sure way to ensure that he won't be trustworthy. However, once he violates your trust, you can just about be sure that he will do it again. For instance, a woman who cheats with a married man shouldn't be surprised when he turns around and cheats on her. If you instinctively don't trust a man, there are probably some very good reasons that your subconscious is picking up on.

On the other hand, a man who is jealous of you does not love you more than one who is not jealous. In fact, a jealous man does not love you at all—he wants to possess you. Young fatherless women especially confuse jealousy with love. Ways of possessing a woman might include convincing her that her needs and wants don't exist or are not important, or taking away her identity as an individual.

Why do women stay with jealous men and why do men behave that way even when they realize it is destructive? Novelist James Lee Burke comments, "Most women have a level of trust in the men whom they love that men seldom earn or deserve. As a rule, we do not appreciate that level of trust until it's destroyed."[4]

Unprovoked or overly jealous behavior can be a strong indicator of a possible abusive personality. It is a warning sign that you need to recognize.

Jealousy usually indicates some significant underlying issues like fear of abandonment or a controlling personality. These issues need to be addressed by a professional.

Abusive and Controlling

Many women who come from abusive homes or who have low self-esteem or a poor self-image unconsciously gravitate toward abusive relationships. They are easy targets because they don't have the ability to recognize healthy or unhealthy relationships. And girls from fatherless homes often find themselves in abusive situations by default—they had no guidelines to follow and their need for love was never fulfilled as it should have been. Men with abusive tendencies are adept at picking up on the vulnerabilities of women from these backgrounds.

There is a strong correlation between controlling behaviors and abuse. Battering and abusive conduct are learned behaviors in men. If a man had a father who exhibited those character traits or has a family history of abuse, he is more likely to be abusive, violent, and sexually aggressive. Research shows that over 50 percent of all women will experience some form of violence from their intimate partners.[5] Some 30 percent of women murdered in the U.S. are murdered by their husbands, ex-husbands, or boyfriends.[6]

We typically think of physical violence or emotional cruelty when we think of abuse. But another way men can be controlling in a relationship, especially with a woman who struggles with unresolved issues, is to allow or enable her to act a certain way ("You deserve to take drugs because you were molested as a child"). He then uses those behaviors as a way to control her by throwing them in her face ("If you weren't taking so many drugs, we could have a better relationship" or "You don't deserve anything better because you're a drug addict" or "You are lucky to have me because you have children by another man"). This form of passive-aggressive manipulation is easy for a woman to buy into because of the guilt she feels.

This kind of man is also always on the lookout for her faults. If he can't find any, he will make some up. For instance, the house is clean but a toy or a sock is left out, and he blows it out of proportion: "Can't you even keep the house clean? You're so lazy."

If you feel like you have to walk around on eggshells all the time, or are being accused of things you did not do or intend, you might be heading toward an abusive relationship. If a man has ever hit you (even once), verbally abused you, or sexually assaulted you, you are in an abusive relationship. It doesn't matter what he says or how often he apologizes or how much you want him to change; you are in a dangerous, no-win situation that will continue to escalate. If you have children, they are not only in danger but your sons are learning to act abusively toward women and your daughters learn to see abuse as normal and to expect to be treated that way by men.

If you find yourself in a situation like this, you must find the courage to extricate yourself immediately. There are many organizations, social agencies, shelters, and programs that can help you with your situation, but you must make the first step by contacting them. Secrecy is one of the most effective tools of evil. Not speaking about abuse keeps women and children in the darkness of bondage and perpetuates that cycle onto future generations.

Predators

Our moral failure lies in the frailty of our vision and not in our hearts. Our undoing is in our collective willingness to trust those whom we shouldn't, those who invariably used our best instincts against us.

James Lee Burke, *Crusader's Cross*

With the advent of the Internet, a whole new realm of options opened up for several types of male predators, including the sexual predator and the parasite. There is something deceptively attractive about these types of men. They make women feel needed.

The most astonishing thing I've discovered while researching this book is how many women in our country (young and old) genuinely seem to suffer from a variety of emotional struggles—everything from poor self-image, low self-esteem, poor body image, lack of confidence, or a desperate hunger for attention and affection. From all outward appearances, I would have never suspected that a significant portion of the female population secretly suffered from these and other problems.

Author and speaker Angela Thomas eloquently sums up so many women's struggles: "I have a friend who sits in the ashes of a passionless life.... Other women sit in the ashes of deep woundedness... the addictions of a parent, the distance of a father, the anger of a mom, abandonment, rape, incest, emotional or mental abuse. These women grieve the pain of their memories, curse the ugliness of their scars, and cry for the lives that have been stolen from them."[7]

Men who are predatory in nature learn about these vulnerabilities in women early in life and use them for their own self-gratification. Predators use and manipulate women to satisfy their need for money, sex, and power. These men typically hate women—although they are seldom without one. They are adept at manipulation and can spot needy women and children from a mile away. They figuratively, and sometimes literally, ravage women and then toss them away like used tissue.

Often these types of men specifically target single mothers (or fatherless girls) for a variety of reasons. One reason is that they are easier targets. In the movie *About a Boy*, Hugh Grant stars as a self-centered bachelor who specifically targets single "mums" for his sexual peccadilloes. He chooses them because he believes they are easy to lie to, they want to believe in him, and they are desperate.

When asked what women need to be aware of regarding men, one single mom stated it this way:

> The biggest danger signal that popped into my mind is the man that wants to rescue (especially the single mom) or is overzealous in wanting to protect and nurture her and her kids. It has been my experience that these types of men are generally pedophiles and abusers. As single moms (and women in general) we feel used up. Everyone, even our own children, seem to know we are so exhausted that we are in survival mode most of the time. Predators can see this from a mile away—from bosses who will work you as much as possible for as little money as possible, to the guy at the local mini-mart. It makes us an extremely easy target. People who are living in desperation are easy targets for anything.

The biggest problem with being involved with men like those we profiled in this chapter is that not only do you suffer but your children are the ones who ultimately suffer the consequences of your choices and decisions. Because of the relationship modeled for them, they grow up thinking it is normal behavior to abuse women and children (or be abused) and to abandon families. This perpetuates the cycle into the next generation, creating more single mothers, fatherless children, and future generations of abusers.

5

Speaking Your Man's Language

Marrying a man is like buying something you've been admiring for a long time in a shop window. You may love it when you get it home, but it doesn't always go with everything else in the house.

Jean Kerr, "The Ten Worst Things About a Man"

Horses have their own style of communicating. Men have their own style of communicating as well. Successful horse whisperers understand that you have to speak the horse's "language" if you want to relate effectively with him. Women who connect and converse successfully with men understand that because of women's superior verbal skills, they must speak a man's "language" if they want to interact effectively with him.

Horses don't speak in audible "words," but they do communicate with body language, voice, and, some believe, even "telepathy." Horses also communicate using their highly developed senses. Their hearing is extremely sensitive; their sense of smell is far superior to humans (a stallion can smell a mare in season up to five miles away). Their eyesight is poor compared to humans. But the placement of the eyes on the head allows them to see far more than humans can. Their eyesight is monocular so they can focus on two different scenes at one time. Horses can see in the dark. Their skin is so sensitive that the mere lighting of a fly on their croup can cause the whole body to shake it off. Their nostrils and taste glands are so connected with one another that a stallion can actually taste and savor the mare's scent. All these senses work together to form a unique communications system.

It only makes sense that if we, as humans, are to communicate effectively with horses, we should learn as much as possible about the ways horses "speak" with one another. Then we can begin to communicate effectively, without undue force, with our horses.

Four Dreaded Words

I instantly get a sense of dread whenever my wife says, "WE NEED TO TALK." And if my wife *and* daughter approach me together with that statement, I want to run and hide. Because men are not very proficient at verbal communication, we are suspicious or even fearful of it. An emotional discussion can easily turn into a BHD (Big Hairy Deal). Frankly, it's easier just to keep quiet or ignore the issue.

A woman needs to learn a man's "language" if she wants to communicate effectively with him. His natural fear of opening up and becoming vulnerable must be overcome with trust in order to communicate effectively with him.

Men often do not use audible words but communicate through body language instead. They are uncomfortable with verbal conversations and seldom talk face-to-face but instead prefer to sit or stand next to each other, side by side. When they talk, males talk about doing things, not about relationships. They use their senses to communicate as well. Men are very visual and evaluate much information through their eyes, ears, and noses. A man's role for thousands of years was as a hunter to provide food. This developed his eyesight and hearing and gave him the ability to sit quietly and focus on one thing for long periods of time. This development of his ocular senses explains why certain images and movements attract his attention—things like attractive women, video games, powerful automobiles, and fast-moving sports. This skill also allowed him to shut things out so that they would not distract him from the task at hand.

Let's look at some ways men and women communicate differently, and then explore some ways women can effectively bridge those differences.

How Do Women Communicate?

In many ways women are much smarter than men and we men know it. That scares us. It's eerie how women sometimes know what we are thinking—even when *we* don't. And if a man has done anything wrong, forget it! He might as well confess his sins and beg forgiveness because there's no way he can hide it from a woman.

This probably starts with a boy's mother. All moms are mind readers. It's a power that gets passed down generationally from female to female. I have watched my wife subtly teach our daughter little mental telepathy–type tricks over the years. And I've watched my daughter unconsciously emulate her mother's intuitiveness without even knowing it. Now that she's getting more confident using this powerful tool, it's kind of fun watching her confound, confuse, and even manipulate the young men she dates as she bends them to her will without them knowing what's going on. It's sort of like watching a spider spin a web around her unsuspecting prey.

Communication is a very important, yet very difficult task between two independent individuals and genders with differing experiences, values, and perceptions. However, women have much more highly developed communication skills than men. Girls develop the right side of the brain faster than boys. This leads to earlier talking, larger vocabulary, better pronunciation, earlier reading, and better memory.

Boys tend to develop the left side of the brain faster than girls, leading to better visual-spatial-logical skills, perceptual skills, math skills, problem solving, building skills, and puzzle-solving skills.

Females hear better, see better, have a better sense of smell and touch, and are able to read emotions on a person's face more easily than men. This gives a woman a big advantage with interpersonal communication skills because she can pick up on nonverbal cues much more readily than a man will.

The corpus callosum is a bundle of nerves which connect the left and right hemispheres of the brain. A female has a larger corpus callosum than a male. This allows the two hemispheres of her brain to function better together and communicate back and forth more easily than a male's. Magnetic resonance imaging (MRI) and other brain-scanning studies have shown that during verbal communication oftentimes both hemispheres of a woman's brain light up at the same time. When they stop talking, usually one hemisphere or the other will stay "lit," indicating brain wave activity. Conversely, when men speak, typically only one side or the other of their brain will light up. When they stop talking, both sides generally go blank.[1]

Remember all those times you've asked your husband or boyfriend what he's thinking and he says, "Nothing"? Well, he was probably telling the truth. Males have the unremarkable ability to shut off our brains and just "be." It often happens when we zone out watching television, especially during commercials, or when driving the car. If you've ever had to sit quietly for long periods of time while hunting, you understand that this is a good ability to have.

Women also generally have a much larger vocabulary than men and typically use about two to three times as many words each day as men do. In fact, as amazing as this is to me, women *like* to talk—they actually enjoy it! They talk to process information and their feelings. They talk with each other to be closer and more intimate.

Men do things (physical activities) together. When I am with my buddies, we are *doing* things, not *talking* about them. If I were to just sit around and talk to someone, it would feel like I was seeing a counselor.

All this leads many men to feel at a big disadvantage when communicating verbally. In fact, it can be quite intimidating for a man to sit face-to-face with someone who is so much more skilled at an attribute than he is. I can remember telling my wife more than once, "Just because you can express yourself better than I can does not mean you are always right." Of course she *was* right, but it was frustrating nonetheless.

How Do Men Communicate?

There are 2 theories to arguing with a woman . . . neither works.

Will Rogers

An important factor in communicating with men is to understand how men think. Because men are not as polished with verbal skills, they do not place as much value on them. Perhaps this is why men have a tendency to not adhere to their promises and why a man's actions always speak louder than his words. Judge a man by what he does, not what he says. My wife has stated that while some (probably many) of the things I have said to her over the years have made her angry, when she stopped and thought about it, my actions always showed her that I love her.

With men, actions speak louder than words, but women seem to believe words over actions. So from a woman's perspective, what a man says oftentimes has more credibility than how he actually acts. Men, being more performance oriented, tend to judge by actions and not by what a person says. It would be in your best interest to test a man's character by watching how he acts, not just going by what he says. Over and over I see women who hang their hat on the head of a loser. They say, "But he *says* he wants to straighten out and get married!" or "He *says* he loves me!" Unfortunately his actions do not support his claims. Judge a man by what he does, not what he says.

Another example of women valuing verbal communication over actions is found in observing what hurts them deeply. Many divorced women whose husbands cheated on them or

80

Communication Needs[2]

MEN

- Sincerity—They want to know that the topic is important to you.
- Simplicity—They want to hear the simple facts and get to the point.
- Sensitivity—They will open up better at the right time and the right place.
- Stability—They want to keep their composure and not fall apart during communication.

WOMEN

- Attention—They want their mate's full attention when they speak.
- Agreement—They want no arguments to break down the walls between them and their mates.
- Appreciation—They want their mates to value them and their roles.
- Appointments—They want their mates to honor the time and place for communication.

were addicted to pornography have reported to me that the lies their husbands told hurt them much more deeply than the actual actions he performed. I suspect most men, if the situation were reversed, would be more disturbed by their wives' actions than any lies they may have told.

Men also tend to not be able to articulate their feelings very well. In fact, most men are not comfortable dealing with or identifying their emotions. Men are awkward and embarrassed in emotional situations. It's why many women get their way when they resort to tears.

Men also have to think about their feelings before they verbalize them. Many times during a discussion, my wife will expect an immediate answer to her question or comment. I often have to tell her, "Wait, I don't know how I feel about that. Let me think about it for a while and see if I can figure out what I am *really* feeling." Sometimes it takes days for me to be able to sort through everything and come to a decision about how I think and feel about a subject.

Women can talk, feel, and think all at the same time. Men can't. Again, men are not designed to be able to use the two hemispheres of the brain simultaneously as proficiently as women. And so, during an argument, men may clam up or even leave without coming to a solution. It doesn't mean they don't care or don't want to resolve the situation; their brains literally overload and have to shut down to process their feelings. If you force them beyond this point, you will notice they often respond in anger and frustration. When overstimulated, many men eventually just tune their women out. Women complain that men do not listen, but sometimes it is just because we have been fed too much information and can't process anything more.

That brings up an interesting point: are men less sensitive than women? Maybe, but I don't think it is because men care about things any less than women do; they've just been taught not to express themselves as openly. Men consider complaining or having problems a sign of weakness—if he can't fix his own problems, then he is somehow less a man. Consequently, he tends to not express himself, sometimes to the point of not even letting his needs be known.

Also, men express themselves differently than women do. When men speak to each other, it is generally to establish authority or control, to determine a pecking order or chain of command. Men verbally communicate to exchange information—typically only the pertinent facts. They tend to joke about their problems and concerns or use horseplay to minimize them. Each man understands what the other is really saying, yet it might make no sense to a woman.

Why We Talk

While women like to talk about feelings and emotions, men like to think problems through to an action that provides a solution. Men talk to problem-solve.

For instance, if one of our female friends or ministry volunteers has a personal issue, my philosophy is that it's none of my business unless she asks my opinion. But my wife and all the other women freely offer their advice and opinions. As a man I would be offended if a male friend offered me unsolicited advice—I would feel like he did not respect me and felt I couldn't solve my own problems.

Women draw closer and become more intimate by conversing with their friends and lovers. Men don't communicate this way, so they can't figure out why women are continually talking. Women like to talk to each other about their problems. But, as a man, when my wife talks to me about her problems, I interpret it as a request for advice, and respond with a solution. Of course when I do this, she often feels as if I'm not really "listening." I think I'm being supportive, because men don't talk to each other about their troubles unless they really want a solution. To a man, talking about problems is just complaining. He doesn't realize that a woman is simply trying to establish intimacy—inviting him to share himself with her. Consider sharing your problems with your girlfriends instead, unless you genuinely want to solve a problem. Understand that if you are trying to "get closer" to your man this way, it will probably fail. Men do not establish intimacy that way, and it will likely just lead to more frustration for both of you.

If as a woman you can get your man to open up and talk about his needs, problems, and concerns without him feeling like he's less a man, he will be eternally grateful to you. However, *never* use that information against him during an argument. If you do, it will damage his trust in you. And while I understand that women process information by discussing it with other women, you should know that men feel this is a breach of confidentiality. If you discuss marital or personal issues with your girlfriends, or tell them something vulnerable or embarrassing about him, he will be more than a little peeved about it.

To women, intimacy means closeness. To men, it means vulnerability. Relationships in general and intimacy in particular are all about taking down your defenses and leaving yourself open. That means trusting people enough to give them the power to emotionally injure you, which is absolutely contrary to a man's nature.

Ten Keys to Successful Communication with a Man

So what are some good tips for communicating with men? After all, men are always the last to know when communication is a problem—probably because no one ever tells them.

Give Him Space

One strategy that works well with men is to tell them something you want their feedback on and then ask them to think about it for a day before answering. This takes much of the

Differences Between Men and Women[3]

MEN

- A man's sense of self is defined through his ability to achieve results through success and accomplishment. Achieve goals and prove his competence and feel good about himself.
- To feel good about themselves, men must achieve goals by themselves.
- For men, doing things by themselves is a symbol of efficiency, power, and competence.
- In general, men are more interested in objects and things rather than people and feelings.
- Men rarely talk about their problems unless they are seeking "expert" advice; asking for help when you can do something yourself is a sign of weakness.
- Men are more aggressive than women; more combative and territorial.
- Men's self-esteem is more career-related.
- Men feel devastated by failure and financial setbacks; they tend to obsess about money much more than women.
- Men hate to ask for information because it shows they are failures.

WOMEN

- Women value love, communication, beauty, and relationships.
- A woman's sense of self is defined through their feelings and the quality of their relationships. They spend much time supporting, nurturing, and helping each other. They experience fulfillment through sharing and relating.
- Personal expression, in clothes and feelings, is very important. Communication is important. Talking, sharing and relating is how a woman feels good about herself.
- For women, offering help is not a sign of weakness but a sign of strength; it is a sign of caring to give support.
- Women are very concerned about issues relating to physical attractiveness; changes in this area can be as difficult for women as changes in a man's financial status.
- When men are preoccupied with work or money, women interpret it as rejection.

stress and pressure off him to respond immediately—especially to an emotionally charged issue. I often find myself saying no to any and everything when thrust into an immediate-response kind of situation. I guess I'd rather be cautiously rude than take a chance on being wrong. For instance, if my wife surprises me with an impromptu request to go shopping for home décor, I will probably be less than thrilled. But if she prepares me ahead of time and let's me mull it over for a day, I might be slightly more enthusiastic. By prepping me ahead of time and telling me something like, "I sure would like your help with this decision," she ensures my cooperation. Interestingly, she always seems to "coincidently" schedule a visit to the hardware store right after her store visit. That makes me happy.

Simplify

Learn to simplify the conversation. If you talk to your man like you do your girlfriends, he will just stop listening. Most men have relatively short attention spans. If you haven't gotten to the point within thirty seconds or so, their attention will begin to drift. It's not that your man is not interested in you; he's just not interested in all the details.

One Topic at a Time, Please

Stick to one topic at a time and let a man know when you're changing topics. I tell moms to speak in sound bites to their boys. This is probably not bad advice when speaking to men either.

Perhaps the greatest communication gift my wife has given my son and me is to let us know when she is changing subjects during a conversation. In the past, my wife would move on to several different subjects while I was still trying to process the first one. If I was lucky, she would eventually circle around and end up back on the original topic where I would be just getting up to speed. Unfortunately, I had missed all of the other stuff she had talked about in between. I found this especially confusing if she talked about two different people with the same name during the conversation.

Now, she and my teenage daughter have both learned to say, "New topic!" whenever they are switching gears, and it cues us guys to drop the former topic and concentrate on the new one. This is a great relief to the males in our family.

Be Consistent

Consistency is very important when communicating with men. My wife's brother owns a ranch with several horses that my niece rides competitively. One day he and I were talking about horse training. He told me that he thinks horses are similar to autistic three-year-old children. He clarified that statement by saying that a trainer must do everything the same way, every single time, or it throws the horse off track. Any changes confuse them and cause them to lose focus. Consistency is the key. But he also believes that most horses (like most men) are starved for affection and desperately want to please you. As long as they understand what you want, they will go out of their way to please you.

Later that evening I was talking with his wife. She was making pudding for her father. Out of the blue, she made the comment, "I try to keep his schedule and everything he does consistent. As he has gotten older, any changes throw him off track."

I'm not necessarily making a correlation between men, horses, and autistic children (and I'm certainly not denigrating any of them either), but the parallels of these two independent conversations within hours of each other were striking. Women need to be consistent in their behavior with men. If you are inconsistent, it throws us off—we don't know what is expected of us.

Say What You Really Mean

Men are much more literal in their conversations than women. For instance when he asks, "What's wrong?" and you say, "Nothing," you might mean, *There is a problem, and if you really loved me, you'd stay and ask me more questions.* But he takes you at your word and figures you just need some time to yourself to work through your problems like he does. Likely, he will walk away to honor your request, like he would appreciate you doing if the situation were reversed.

Sometimes when I ask my wife what's wrong and she replies with "Nothing," because I'm an intelligent, sensitive guy, I know there really is something bothering her. But because I know if I dig deeper, I'm going to end up being in trouble about something, and that makes me pretty nervous, I back off and mind my own business. And then she gets mad at me for not caring enough to try to help her with whatever's bothering her. That confuses me.

From a woman's perspective, when you ask him questions like, "How was work today?" you are probably trying to stimulate conversation. When he answers with a one-word response, what he's really saying is, "Please leave me alone." If you keep peppering him with questions, he will get up and leave so that he doesn't get mad at you.

88

Give Him a Problem to Solve

Men love to problem-solve and are often able to disassociate themselves emotionally from the issue under those pretenses. You can get much more cooperation from a man if you present your concerns as a problem that you'd like his help solving. Rather than nagging him about an issue that's troubling you, say something like, "Honey, I have a problem that I'd really like to get your help with." He will be much more willing to address the problem under those circumstances.

Get Physical

Since men are action oriented, take a walk or go hiking, play a round of golf, or even drive on a deserted highway together (so he's not distracted by traffic) when you want to talk with your man. Talk with him while he's working on a household project or fixing the car (unless he needs to concentrate or is frustrated with what he is doing—remember men generally don't multitask very well). He will enjoy your company and you can hand him the tools he needs—that is always appreciated! A physical activity allows a man to process information more easily. It allows his mind to focus on something and be free to listen instead of looking for solutions. It seems to take away some of the discomfort we feel in face-to-face discussions. You will find he is much more open to having conversations when he is doing something than asking him to sit down and talk.

Timing Is Everything

If you bombard him with complaints the minute he walks in the door from a hard day at work, he's not likely to be willing to listen. He needs time to unwind and recharge his batteries. Unfortunately, most women have been anxiously waiting to unload the burdens they have accumulated all day long. Oftentimes, giving him a half hour to change clothes and decompress will do the trick. When he gets home, say, "Honey, after you get a chance to unwind a little, I'd love to run a few things past you. Let me know when you are ready— no big deal." It's important for him to understand that it's not a big deal. That way he will not be stressed out while he is unwinding.

When your man is watching television (especially sports) or reading the newspaper, it is not a good time to try to engage him. Men do not multitask very well. If you ask him to concentrate on more than one thing at a time, you will likely both end up frustrated. Watching sports on TV is a downtime of release for men—it's a time they recharge their batteries. When I am watching a game on television, my wife will usually say, "When you have a break in the game, can you come and see me? I need to get your opinion on something."

That prompting allows me to prepare myself mentally for a verbal discussion. That probably sounds silly to most women, but men do not transition into a talking mode as easily as women do. I almost have to psyche myself up for a conversation. Sometimes we feel blindsided if we are forced to engage in an important or emotional discussion when we are unprepared. You can use that to your advantage, but keep these two things in mind: 1) when men are caught unawares or unprepared, it can be frightening to them; and 2) men often react to fear with anger. Probably neither emotion is the best frame of mind for having a discussion.

Fight Fair

Men forgive easier and are more easily corrected in their behaviors with positive feedback than women are.

Dr. Laura Schlessinger, *The Proper Care and Feeding of Husbands*

Men and women argue differently. You cannot take to heart much of what a man verbalizes when he is upset. He doesn't think about what comes out of his mouth, especially in the heat of the moment. Unfortunately for men, women do.

Frank Pittman says it this way in his book *Man Enough*: "When we men have any important message to deliver, we deliver it as logically and unemotionally as possible. We know that what we say when we're angry should be ignored, and our friends do us the favor of ignoring it. We often wish women would do the same."[4]

Women typically think about what they say—and then think a lot about what is said to them. Men often do not, and as a result they say things they do not mean and later regret.[5]

Again, because women are so much more proficient verbally, they have a big advantage in arguments. Most men do not like verbal confrontations—we know we are doomed to lose any verbal argument with a female. A woman who uses that advantage ruthlessly to win an argument no matter the cost is a great source of frustration to a man. It would be like him physically intimidating you with his greater size every time he wanted to make a point. If you've ever experienced that, you know how scary that can be. A woman's sharp tongue can be just as scary to a man as his dominant physical strength is to her.

My wife tells me that women have a lot of internal dialogue that goes on in their heads. That's why they get upset and angry about things that a man often doesn't even know he's done. They stew about little things that pile up and eventually fester. I can tell you that, at least from my experience, men do not have a lot of internal dialogue. What you see is usually what you get.

You can help your husband with communication skills by understanding that he just does not enjoy talking as much as you do. Men do stuff together for hours without speaking and can be perfectly content. For instance, if a man reaches over and grabs a handful of potato chips, other men just assume he's hungry—he doesn't have to say he's hungry, explain why he's hungry, or tell us about the struggles he has maintaining his weight. And if he's eating for some reason other than hunger, we really don't want to know.

When I am feeling agitated or have a problem to solve, I would much rather pace or take a walk than discuss the problem—at least until I've figured out a solution. Or until I've nailed down what it is that's really bothering me and outlined the parameters of the problem. Once I get my arms around the problem, I might feel like talking about it to figure out a solution, but it's just as likely I won't, because by then it's not so much of an issue anymore.

Speak Plainly

Men and women can learn to communicate, but it takes effort and patience from both genders. Help him understand that verbal communication is an important part of the relationship to you. Let him know up front what you expect of

Why Men and Women
Aren't Always on the Same Page

1. THINGY (thing-ee) n.
   Female: Any part under a car's hood.
   Male: The strap fastener on a woman's bra.
2. VULNERABLE (vul-ne-ra-bel) adj.
   Female: Fully opening up one's self emotionally to another.
   Male: Playing football without a cup.
3. COMMUNICATION (ko-myoo-ni-kay-shon) n.
   Female: The open sharing of thoughts and feelings with one's partner.
   Male: Leaving a note before taking off on a fishing trip with the boys.
4. COMMITMENT (ko-mit-ment) n.
   Female: A desire to get married and raise a family.
   Male: Trying not to hit on other women while out with this one.
5. ENTERTAINMENT (en-ter-tayn-ment) n.
   Female: A good movie, concert, play, or book.
   Male: Anything that can be done while drinking a favorite recreational beverage.
6. FLATULENCE (flach-u-lens) n.
   Female: An embarrassing by-product of indigestion.
   Male: A source of entertainment, self-expression, male bonding.
7. MAKING LOVE (may-king luv) n.
   Female: The greatest expression of intimacy a couple can achieve.
   Male: Call it whatever you want, just as long as we do it.
8. REMOTE CONTROL (ri-moht kon-trohl) n.
   Female: A device for changing from one TV channel to another.
   Male: A device for scanning through all 375 channels every 5 minutes.

Anonymous email

him so you can both relax. Remind him *often* that you just need to be heard—you are not looking for a solution. Tell him that at the beginning of the discussion so that he can switch off his "problem-solving" mode. Say something like, "Honey, I'm really not looking for a solution to this issue, I just need to talk about it so I can process it. Thank you for listening to me—it really makes me feel loved."

Also, communicate to him that when he shares his thoughts and feelings with you, it makes you feel closer to him. A good way to help him understand how important this is to you is to equate it to a form of sexual foreplay. That will probably help him understand the importance of talking and sharing.

Speak plainly to your man. Men are very poor mind readers, and for all practical purposes they aren't able to read between the lines very well either. If you hint around a subject hoping he will get it on his own, you are setting yourself up for disappointment. Men hate trying to guess what you want, or worse, what is wrong. Tell him up front and directly what you want and how you feel. He doesn't need all the details and who said what.

Women like to drop subtle hints, but men as a rule aren't very subtle. Sometimes you need to be blunt. Asking a man if he notices anything different after you've gotten your hair cut and styled is setting him up for failure. You'd be better off asking him how your new hairstyle makes you look. At least he knows how he's supposed to answer that question.

Most men are more than willing to do whatever will make you happy if you are direct with them so they know what is expected.

A woman, with her superior communication skills, can be a big help to her man (and her relationship) by helping and guiding him to learn to communicate better instead of being agitated by his lack of skills in this area (or using it to her advantage to "win" all the time). Hopefully, your husband is just as patient with you in areas that you might not be as adept as he is (such as reading a map or field-dressing a deer), and so you complement him best by patiently helping him with areas he struggles with, such as verbal communication and emotion identification. It's all part of being a well-functioning team—using each other's strengths to complement the other partner's weaknesses.

6

Power Tools for Women

Men are not very good at loving, but they are experts at admiring and respecting; the woman who goes after their admiration and respect will often come out better than she who goes out after their love.

Florence King, *"Spinsterhood Is Powerful"*

Men are really pretty simple creatures—at least we are much less complicated than women give us credit for being. We deeply desire to please you. My wife's contentment means the world to me. If she is unhappy and grumbling about her life, I'm pretty miserable—I feel inadequate. But when I hear her humming or singing while doing some simple task around the house, I know she is content and it makes me feel good that I have done my job as a man and husband. I am validated and empowered as a man.

When a woman understands how to *effectively* use the influence God gave her, there are not many areas of a man's life that she cannot have a positive effect over (provided a man is willing to be influenced). Let's look at some positive tools that a woman can use to influence her man to be more than he could ever accomplish without her.

Positive Tools for Influencing Your Man

Respect and Admiration

The two most powerful tools a woman has to influence a man are respect and admiration. He will do most anything to get genuine appreciation, respect, admiration, and pride from you. In fact, a man needs respect and admiration from his woman even more than he does her love. These desires are more subconscious than his physical needs and, when used properly, even more of a powerful motivating force. If you asked a group of men whether they'd rather live their whole lives being loved but disrespected or being respected but unloved, most would overwhelmingly choose the respected option.

If a man's wife does not believe in him or does not respect him or is continually dissatisfied, he will feel hopeless with no reason to go forward or attempt any new challenges. He will feel, "What's the point?" He will feel . . . unloved. Unfortunately, if your husband is not getting the kind of affirmation, support, and encouragement he needs at home, he'll probably seek it elsewhere. There are many individuals and businesses out there that prey upon your husband's need to feel good about himself as a man.

Respect means a great deal to men. The concept of respect is intrinsic to a man's soul. That means it is important that he not only receive respect from you but that he respects you as well. Men who don't respect their women become contemptuous of them pretty quickly. They are then generally not interested in honoring or loving them in the ways a woman needs.

Typically, most men respect their mother and that's why that bond is so strong. If a man respects you as a woman, he will be much more amenable to your influence. (His respect for his mother is why her influence is so strong.) Unfortunately, there are several things that cause men to lose respect for women. It starts with how easily she initially goes to bed with him in the beginning of their relationship. That seems a bit provincial in today's climate, but it's still true nonetheless.

Also, if a woman allows herself to be pushed around by a man, she runs the risk of him losing respect for her. A woman has to advocate for her rights and not allow someone to impose his will upon her. I'm about a foot taller than my wife and a lot bigger and more physically imposing. But she's never been afraid of sticking her chin out and giving me what-for if I tried to intimidate her. She holds her ground on the issues that are important to her and she feels strongly about. I might not always like it, but I respect that about her.

If a woman gives in to a man's will too easily, he might not respect her. If she always sacrifices her desires for his, he might treat her like a doormat. Women are generally nurturers and often put others' needs before their own. Especially early in the relationship, a woman *wants* to meet his needs and even serve him—it's in her nature and she wants to make him happy. But when a habit of being overly sensitive to his needs is established early in the relationship, it can often spiral downward into a disrespectful, one-sided relationship. Instead, he needs to feel like he overachieved with the woman he married and is grateful she chose him.

So how can a woman encourage a man even when his actions are not worthy of respect? Can a woman, through her actions and attitude, change a man's behavior? And if so, what comes first—her respect or his behavior change?

Here's what one woman said after attending one of our seminars:

> I have been praying about how to be a better parent, and I felt like God put it on my heart that the best gift I could give our children was a stronger marriage. Here is one specific way your seminar helped my parenting and marriage: Learning that men need respect as much or more than they need love. I have a tendency to criticize and correct my husband. The Lord had put it on my heart to stop doing this, but I was having a difficult time breaking the habit. As you spoke about this at your workshop, I felt the Spirit chastise me for treating my husband poorly. He never criticizes me! It's been a week now, and I have learned to change my thoughts and words. My husband doesn't know you but he thanks you.

Your man needs respect and admiration from you as much as you need love and honor from him. Men need this from their women, not because of our pride, but because secretly most of us feel inadequate. Males have very fragile egos. Even the most competent and self-assured of us (on the outside) secretly feel like impostors—we think we are going to be "found out." When you criticize him, or good-naturedly make fun of him (especially in public), or try to control things that he is responsible for, it is interpreted as a sign of disrespect, and it humiliates him. The book of Proverbs says, "An excellent wife is the crown of her husband, but she who causes shame is like rottenness in his bones" (Prov. 12:4 NKJV). Not having confidence in your husband to perform a task or trying to tell him how to do something he is responsible for is implying that he is incompetent and causes him shame. Accusing him of being incompetent (even inadvertently) is as devastating and hurtful to him as his calling you fat and ugly would be to you.

Some women may have lost respect for their husband because of his past actions. Others of you may be caught in the vicious cycle of not feeling loved by your husband so you withhold respect for him, which causes him to withhold his love even more, and so on, until you both despise each other. By recognizing that your disrespect (intended or not) might cause him to withhold love, you can help stop this cycle before it gets beyond repair. Discussing with your husband that your feeling loved by him is as important to you as him feeling respected by you is a good step toward understanding and fulfilling each other's needs.

Believe in Him

Being believed in by someone is a powerful motivator. When someone believes in you, it tends to make you believe in yourself. As a basketball coach, one of my highest priorities is to help my players understand that I believe in them—that I have faith in them. When they recognize that, their trust in me grows and their self-confidence blooms. It motivates them and inspires them to greater achievements. They are willing to do things that they never would have attempted without my belief in them. One player's dad shook his head in wonder and told me, "Those girls would run through a brick wall for you if you asked them to." And they would. But it's because they know I believe in them, and they trust that I always have their best interests at heart. They know I would never do anything to intentionally hurt them. I have earned that trust by proving to them over and over again that I care about them and that every decision I make is with them in mind.

But it is even more powerful when a man's woman believes in him. A woman's support and influence can make a man strong and fearless. Your man needs a cheerleader. The world is tough enough on him. He needs someone who believes in him.

I asked my sister Terry what she felt was the biggest factor in her influencing her husband toward being the man God had created him to be. She said something that surprised me. She told me that she let him go for his dreams. Her husband, Scott, is arguably the most successful voice actor in Hollywood today, certainly the most active. When I asked if that was difficult when he came to her as a young man with crazy dreams, she replied, "They didn't seem that way at the time."

I probed further. "Terry, most women, if their husband came to them and said, 'I'm going to make a living being a voice for cartoon characters and movie trailers,' they would have thought that was a pretty crazy dream."

She laughed and replied, "You know, when I let him go for his dreams, it was amazing to watch God work. It was so obvious that he was behind everything, that it made it easy for me to be supportive. I've just always tried to be my husband's biggest cheerleader." Wise words from a very influential woman.

Having a woman believe in him is a powerful need in a man's life. In fact, I am probably married to the woman I am today (for twenty-six years) because on our second date she gave me a card that merely said, "I believe in you." It was the first time in my life that anyone had ever believed in me. Frankly, as I look back, I have no idea what she ever saw in me. I shudder to think of where I might have ended up today without that faith. But without that belief, I would never have achieved my potential as a man, husband, or father.

Stand by Your Man

Many years ago my sister severely scolded me publicly for exhibiting behavior toward her husband that was disrespectful. She was right and I was wrong—way wrong. It was a lesson I have never forgotten. She was not fighting his battles for him. She was defending his honor in a situation where he was not able to without looking bad. Her defense honored my brother-in-law. When I apologized and asked his forgiveness, he was able to garner even more honor through his gracious acceptance. He did not feel the need to have to vindicate himself as he had already been defended.

A woman should not fight a man's battles for him. But there are situations when he needs your support—especially where family is concerned. If a woman is not willing to defend her husband to her relatives, she shouldn't be married to him.

Raise the Bar

You inspire your man by your example and the standards you hold him to. If you conduct your life with integrity, he will be forced to live a life of honor and virtue—at least he will if he wants to stay with you.

Lift him up to a higher standard in life. Not by nagging him, but by encouraging him to be his best. When my wife says things like, "I just know you can do that" or "You're the kind of man who can do anything he sets his mind to," she can rest assured that I will do everything in my power to accomplish that task. And when she expresses her genuine gratitude and admiration when I do accomplish that task, it makes all the effort worthwhile. It also ensures that I will want to do my best the next time she encourages me or asks me to do something.

Build Up His Strengths

Women of influence nurture strengths instead of exploit weaknesses. Most segments of our culture tell us to work on our weaknesses, not our strengths. But that is a form of criticism, not encouragement. Nurturing our areas of strength is encouraging and uplifting.

Instead of focusing on the things your man does wrong, try focusing on the things he does right. Study him carefully to find out what his strengths and weaknesses are. Then help him understand his strengths—his gifts from God. Many people do not know what their strengths are. All of us have been blessed with certain skills and find ourselves lacking in others. Find out where he excels, and help him use and cultivate those strengths to succeed in life. Encourage him to develop those gifts. When we use our God-given gifts to their potential, we lead very fulfilling lives.

Be intentional about understanding what strengths you have that he doesn't, and what strengths he has where you are weak. Embrace your differences. Then use your strengths, without making a big deal out of it, to help him succeed. That's not manipulating him; it is partnering with him to use your strengths to compensate for the areas where he is lacking. God gave you this incredible influence in your man's life to empower him. Power is given by God to serve others, not to enslave or crush them.

The couples who are able to recognize each partner's strengths and weaknesses and then most effectively work together as a team are those couples who are the happiest and most satisfied in their relationships.

Praise

If a man knows his wife is proud of him, he can withstand a lot of slings and arrows from the rest of the world. That's how important you are. There's much wisdom in the statement, "Behind every great man is a great woman." Being proud of your husband and trusting his judgment are two ways that you can show him you respect him.

Building your husband up in public is another way. Tell people how great he is both in front of him and when he's not around—brag about him behind his back. A woman who chooses to honor and respect her man in public even when he doesn't deserve it lifts up both of them. When you do that, you are not glossing over his mistakes, you are inspiring him to a new standard of behavior. Many men reported to me that even if their wives do not build them up to their face, when they brag about them to others, it more than makes up for it. They said it inspired them to step up to the plate to be a good man. Men tend to judge their success in life based on the happiness and respect of their wives. *In most successful marriages, the wife sincerely admires her husband and is not shy about telling him and others about it.*

A trap many women fall into that I think our culture encourages is to expect certain high standards from their husbands *before* giving them respect. To honor your man is a gift you give him and is not based on his performance. Otherwise, it is not honor; it is feedback.

I'm not sure how or when my wife started treating me with respect, but I'm pretty sure I was not at a stage in my maturity where I deserved it. I can tell you that by her telling (and showing) me she admired and respected me, it inspired me to work all the harder to try to live up to her belief in me. I think all men of character will respond the same way.

I overheard a woman make this comment about my wife to a group of other women awhile back: "Suzanne edifies her husband more than any other woman I've ever met!" I nearly popped the buttons off the front of my shirt. It certainly motivated me to respond by giving her the love and honor she craves. And when a woman edifies her man in public, you cannot believe how much credibility it gives a man. I believe it gives him advantages in many circumstances of life that he might not otherwise have. I'm sure that many people hold me at a higher level of esteem than I deserve because of how my wife speaks about me and treats me in public.

If you want to see your husband walk tall, say something like, "I'm so proud of you for doing that." If you want to encourage him during times of struggles, say, "I admire and respect you so much for all you are doing." Tell him you think

Words That Supercharge Your Man

- I have confidence in you. I believe in you.
- You're a real man.
- I appreciate how hard you work to provide for us.
- I just know you can do it.
- I am so proud to be married to you.
- I believe you can do anything you set your mind to.
- I've always admired and respected men like you.
- Thank you for being the kind of man I can count on.
- You are a good man.

he's a good man—he never hears that from anyone else, and it's important. Believe me, he will try his best to get that kind of response from you again. Even if the chore is tough or unpleasant, he will usually stop complaining and grumbling and get on with the task at hand. Few men would risk disappointing their wives after they've been praised for doing something well.

My wife tells me that many women complain about their husbands to their friends. This serves to discourage him and reflects poorly on those women. As one man told me, "Imagine how deflating that would be to know your wife was complaining about and criticizing you to her friends."

And don't worry about him getting a "fat head" from your praise. When you use the qualities of admiration and respect with a man, you are holding him to a nobler vision of life and he will strive to meet those expectations in all areas.

Validation

Validation is also a powerful tool that women can use with men. People who are validated are empowered to grow and change. To validate someone is to give them your approval and confirm their worth and value.

My wife and I were on a speaking tour last spring in the Kenai Peninsula in Alaska. During a seminar break, a woman asked to speak with me. I agreed, somewhat reluctantly since I could tell she had been crying and, like any male, that made me very apprehensive. When we stepped back away from the rest of the crowd, she began to tearfully tell me her story. She said that her husband was an alcoholic and a drug addict. She said that her marriage was in shambles and that she was ready to divorce her husband. She then told me that by some miracle her husband had, quite out of character, attended my fathering workshop the night before. After the workshop, he went home and fell upon his knees and begged his wife's and children's forgiveness. He told them that he had never realized how important he was as a father and husband in their lives, and if they would forgive him, he promised to try harder to change.

Through her sobs she told me it was the first time in many years she had felt validated as a woman and as a wife. She smiled and said, "Now I have hope. Thank you so much for saving my marriage."

She was ready to forgive and start over again all because she felt validated. Her husband was willing to change because his importance had been validated. Validation will smooth over many disagreements. It will make years of hard work and struggles seem worthwhile. And it will make a man, or a woman, *want* to be better; to grow and change.

Forgiveness

Forgiveness is another powerful tool. Forgiveness is an area some women struggle with. Women seem to have much longer memories than men, especially in the area of men's mistakes. My wife can recall at will nearly everything I've ever said or done to hurt her by date, time, and severity of incident for the past twenty-six years. Most of the time, once I get something off my chest, I forget about it and move on. Her willingness to generously forgive my mistakes allows me to learn and grow from them. If my wife were to harbor ill will toward me for extended periods of time, it would cast a pall over our relationship.

Appreciation

All men want to be appreciated. My wife shows me she loves me and appreciates me in a variety of little ways. She screens telephone calls for me so I'm not bothered by telemarketers or other people who would want to waste my time. She protects me from people at events who would like to monopolize my time or want to do me emotional damage. She goes out of her way to buy my favorite foods. And at dinner she always dishes up my food and serves me first before anyone else.

These are small things maybe, but they show me she genuinely appreciates me.

Influence of Other Men

I mentioned earlier that men do not like to be told what to do. But if you can encourage him to meet with other men of character, he will accept advice from them. They also provide an avenue for role modeling and accountability for him. They can influence his perspective in ways a woman cannot. For instance, I can remember on several occasions being told by men I respected things that I would probably never have received well from my wife. Things like, "I think you are off base here. You might reconsider your position on this situation," or "If you do that, here's what will happen . . ."

Some women I know are jealous of their man spending free time away from her, especially when he is with other men. A wife's possessiveness can be smothering to her husband. But if the men he spends time with are worthy of respect, they can provide a huge positive influence on him. They are often able to inspire him to change in ways that no amount of nagging, cajoling, crying, or being angry on your part is capable of doing. When you combine their masculine influence with your intentional positive feminine influence, miraculous things can happen in the life of a man!

What Doesn't Work?

The tools mentioned above are very effective ways to call forth the best in your man. But there are other tools women often resort to that lead to frustration instead of encouragement.

Men prefer honesty to manipulation. If you ask a man to do something in a loving manner, you get much better results than if you use emotional blackmail.

Men hate to be nagged. Even the Bible talks about how unpleasant a man finds this kind of behavior: "a quarrelsome wife is like a constant dripping" (Prov. 19:13). I wonder if some women don't think they have an inherent "right" to nag and voice their complaints after they get married. They just seem to expect men to take it without saying anything in return.

Women nag because it works, but it's exhausting... for both parties. As one woman told me, "Trying to change a man is

She Says	He Thinks
I never get any help around the house.	I have to work harder to afford a maid.
We never have any money.	She thinks I'm not a good provider.
We never go out anymore.	She's never satisfied no matter what I do.
You just don't understand.	What is the problem so I can fix it?
We need to talk.	What did I do wrong now?
You never listen to me!	Did she say something?

frustrating and just plain doesn't work." But what a man often interprets as nagging, a woman would describe as trying to get a man to listen and empathize with her. A man needs to understand what a woman is really trying to say when it feels like she is nagging him. Otherwise, he typically shuts down if he thinks he is being nagged. Good communication skills are critical to helping him understand your needs.

Begging and wheedling can also be used to force a man to do things he doesn't want to do but will cause problems in the long run. Children are adept at using this tactic. They hope to eventually wear you down and get their way if they keep at it long enough. Men suffer this behavior in children, but they find it undignified in women.

Lecturing is similar to nagging. My wife can lecture with the best of them. When she works herself into a frenzy about something, she can go for an hour or more without notes and without winding down. Our children find this spiritual gift of hers particularly galling. They last about a minute before their eyes glaze over. I can typically focus for several minutes

111

before my head too starts to droop. My point is that a man's shorter attention span causes him to shut down if you don't get to the point quickly and concisely.

Yelling and belligerence are negative strategies to use with a man. I witnessed a horrifying spectacle the other day at the supermarket. A large, belligerent woman was bellowing at her mate with the fury of an enraged, red-eyed, snorting, dirt-pawing bull. The man merely stared at the ground. As a man I felt sympathy, shame, and not a little contempt for him. If a woman has that kind of disrespect for her man, no other man will respect him either.

Acting that way may have cowed him into letting her have her way in that circumstance, but it emotionally castrates him and leaves him devoid of love or the desire to cherish his wife.

How to Talk So He'll Listen

Men do not like to be told what to do. A woman can appear to be telling a man what to do even if she doesn't mean it that way. For instance, every time you say, "You should . . ." or "You've got to . . ." or "You need to . . .," you are giving him directives. If he is having a hard time at work, he will be even more sensitive to this and interpret your comments as orders.

You might just be trying to help, but he interprets it as you thinking he needs to be rescued or that he isn't capable of solving the problem on his own. Men hate when women rush in to rescue them without allowing them an opportunity to solve their own problems. Children need to be rescued, not men. Even though men like to solve *your* problems, their compulsion is to solve their own problems without anyone else's help or interference.

When I work with groups of men, I always avoid using the "should" word, as in "You *should* do this." That choice of word tells a man that he is slightly incompetent. I use a less threatening approach like, "I'd like to encourage you to think about this" or "You probably already know this, but have you ever considered this course of action?" Try to use suggestions that he can consider and then either choose or disregard through his own volition.

One woman put it this way:

> I was critical of [my husband] in several areas for a long time. From your class, I learned how much men need respect. It was very hard, but I stopped my habit of being critical. Eventually I had to stop critical thoughts because my thoughts became words. I never told him I was trying to stop being critical. I just did it. After three months, he said to me, "I feel like we have fallen in love all over again." After a while, he became more open concerning parenting issues and spiritual progress. I realized that when I was being critical, I was hindering spiritual growth. He didn't have the space to grow because I was always attacking him.

Likewise if you are always dissatisfied and unhappy, it is very stressful to a man. Again, his mind-set is one of a problem solver. He judges his success by your satisfaction. If he is unable to make you happy, he considers himself a failure.

Being mad or using the silent treatment against him is also often counterproductive. Because he likes to be left alone when he has a problem, he thinks he is respecting you by leaving you alone to solve your issues. When there are serious problems, he'd just as soon not talk about them anyway because he always feels at such a disadvantage. So he might not even notice your use of the silent treatment for a while—of course those dishes and pans being slammed around in the kitchen are a dead giveaway.

Another thing you want to be really careful about is comparing your husband to other men. Just as it is destructive for a man to compare his wife with other women, it is a losing battle to compare him with another man. Men are so competitive that comparing him (even obliquely) to other men can cause him to become angry and resentful or even to shut down and quit trying if he feels overmatched. This is especially true in regard to his work and the income he makes. Complaining about his income is like him complaining about your looks. A woman can do this without even realizing it. That's also why it's extremely important to never criticize him in front of other men—they take it as a sign of weakness if a man's own wife doesn't respect him.

I remember when our children were little, Suzanne was very impressed with how well her friend's husband's business was doing. She talked constantly (in my estimation) about how wonderful he was and how he did this and he did that. My business was young and struggling. Because I was a man and couldn't admit my vulnerabilities, I did not mention my pain and anger to her. But it caused a lot of resentment in me that I'm sure impacted our marriage in other areas. Even though we have since talked about that situation and I realize she was not demeaning me by her praise of another man, I suspect I still hold some resentment toward this man even though he was in no way responsible for my feelings. Interestingly, years later she doesn't even remember being particularly impressed by this man, yet it is something I still feel the sting from.

If you do compare him to other men, make sure it is on good qualities. For instance, if you think he is more manly than your friend's husband, it's probably okay to tell him so. And of course telling him frequently what a good lover you think he is keeps him pumped!

Speaking of which, withholding sex is a dangerous strategy. *But it works*, you might say. *I always get my way when I use it.* It might work in the short term, but it does serious damage to a relationship in the long run. Yes, if a woman withholds sex until she gets her own way, a man will eventually capitulate to her wishes. But a man may just find ways to get even or show his resentment in more destructive ways. Remember that sex to a man is more than just a physical need—it is an emotional requirement. It shows him that he is loved. When you use a fundamental "need" such as sex to manipulate his behavior, it is disrespectful and causes him to feel betrayed and used. We will discuss this in more detail in chapter 8.

These are just a few of the strategies and pitfalls to keep in mind while helping your husband achieve his potential. Some of them will probably work better than others, depending on your relationship and on your husband's unique makeup. Overall, though, if you keep these tips in mind, you'll find your efforts much more effective and your frustration level lower.

7

The First Man
in Every Woman's Life

It is from her father that she begins to infer messages that will linger a lifetime—"I am, or am not, considered by men to be pretty, desirable, valuable, dependent, weak, strong, dim-witted, brilliant"; "Men are, or are not, trustworthy, loving, predatory, dependable, available, dangerous."

Victoria Secunda, *Women and Their Fathers*

If you want to make a difference in your man's life, it is important to understand how and why you chose the man you did. This gives you insight into not only him but yourself as well. Sometimes we learn very valuable insights about others by first learning about ourselves.

Your Father's Influence

Every story has a beginning—a hook that sets up the plotline for the rest of the story. Every woman's life story starts in girlhood. Perhaps the biggest influence on how a woman relates to the opposite sex throughout her life comes in the form of her father.

Fathers have an incredible influence (positive or negative) on nearly every aspect of their daughters' lives. Since every woman reading this book has been impacted by her father (even by his absence), it seems like an appropriate place to begin to discover how and why she goes about choosing the men in her life and relating to them once she enters into a relationship. Your father influenced your self-image, the expectations you have for how a man should treat you, the way you think a man should act, the kind of man you are drawn to, and how you use your influence with a man.

This significant paternal influence was illustrated to me very powerfully recently. My office is in a portion of our family room where the television is located. The other day my teenage daughter, Kelsey, was home ill from school and was watching a modeling program on television. On this episode, as part of their training, the young women hoping to become famous models were taking acting lessons. The acting teacher was instructing them on how to cry on command. She gave them a blank piece of paper and told them to imagine that it was a note from their father saying he was leaving them forever and never wanted to see them again. Every one of the young women instantly burst into tears, some of them sobbing in anguish. The instructor then told them to rip up the paper and release their anger at their fathers. These young women ferociously tore into the papers with almost violent anger. Either these young women were already the best actresses I've ever seen, or it was a gripping testament to the power a father plays in the life of a woman.

Power of Fathers

A father's spoken or written words contain great power. A man's hurtful spoken word can cripple his child's soul for life. Many men and women cherish notes or other blessings they've received from their fathers. One woman spoke of a paper-coated clothes hanger that was her most cherished possession. Her father had written "I love you" on it when she was a little girl. She carried it with her all through college and into her marriage. Elderly people have told me their only regret in life was that they never heard their father say, "I'm proud of you" or "I love you."

God has placed within a daughter's heart the inherent desire, even *need*, to love and respect her father. Even people who have been abused or abandoned by their fathers still *want* to love and respect them. Many girls with fathers in prison still hold them up on a pedestal and refuse to acknowledge their failings. Again, this is a huge power that we need to recognize and encourage men to treat with respect.

Women I surveyed who indicated that they'd had a good, healthy relationship with a loving father provided answers that were calm, confident, and full of joy—like this:

> I had a loving home, grew up with Christ in our family, and accepted Him when I was seven years old. I always knew my parents loved my brother and I, and that they loved each other.

119

My dad was good about playing board games with my brother and I, but was pretty busy. We really became "friends" when I was seventeen years old and my boyfriend (first love) drowned. My dad let me grieve the way I needed to grieve—quietly and in my room most of the time—whereas my mom always wanted me to talk about it. That's when I started to realize for the first time that my dad and I had similar personalities, and therefore could relate to each other better. After I left home and went to college, he started to email me (even though I was only thirty minutes away) on a regular basis. I still have nearly all of those emails saved. That continued through college, graduate school, and my time spent on the mission field. I have since moved back, gotten married and had a baby . . . we now talk on our cell phones nearly every morning on our drive into work.

Women who reported an unhealthy or poor relationship with their fathers responded with comments literally steeped in pain and anguish. Sarah said,

I was a very physical child—I loved sports. My grandmother paid for me to participate because it wasn't important to my parents. In thirteen years of competition, my father did not come to one of my games, meets, or other types of award banquets or recognition services. It was hurtful to be up on stage and not have any of my family there to support me. For most of my early events, my coaches would pick me up and take me home. Other kids thought I was the coach's child because they never saw my parents. It is the reason that I never miss a game or practice for my son and probably why I got into coaching Special Olympics. I never wanted anyone else to feel that they did not have someone there to cheer them on and celebrate the spirit of competition.

And for many women, their fathers are the most important males in their lives. Girls usually stop calling their mothers "Mommy" sometime around the age of eight or nine. But many grown women still call their fathers "Daddy."[1] Lois Mowday says in her book *Daughters without Dads*, "Daddy, for the little girl, is the final authority in approving or disapproving who she is. Many women admitted to me that they had enjoyed a fair amount of affirmation from various people. But if their fathers displayed disapproval, it was as if all the other approval didn't even count. They needed the final okay from daddy."[2]

Role Models

Fathers set a huge role model for their daughters regarding the qualities she looks for in men and the standards she maintains. He is the first man in her life and models how a man should treat a woman, how a man should act, and how a man shows healthy love and affection to a woman. He also sets the standard for how a daughter feels she deserves to be treated by men. He even determines how a girl feels about herself. "A little girl who has her father's love knows what it's like to be unconditionally and completely adored by a man. She knows the feeling of safety that love creates."[3]

Fathers who are active, loving, positive role models in their daughters' lives provide them with the opportunity to use those character traits as a measuring tape for future men in their lives. Dads who model a strong work ethic show young girls how men are supposed to provide for their families. The way a man treats his wife speaks volumes to a girl on how she should expect to be treated and valued by men later in her life. If her father shows that he values her mother as someone worthy of love and respect, a girl will expect that from her husband. If he exhibits a model of abuse or disrespect for her mother, a girl may feel that she deserves to be treated that way as a wife as well.

And if her father shows his daughter love, respect, and appreciation for who she is, she will believe that about herself as a woman, no matter what anyone else thinks.

He also sets the standards a woman expects to live her life by. A woman named Mary told me, "My dad taught me to value honesty, hard work, education, and independence. I tend to have high expectations of myself because I always tried to do better for myself but also for my dad so he would say he was proud of me. I also tend to expect others to live up to my standards and expectations."

Another woman stated, "My dad was always around, usually when I needed him, and was very loving and supportive of my mom—family always came first. So I have those same expectations in my own relationships—I like quality time and expect my husband to be around."

A man who is honest with himself and with others in his life will model to his daughter that a man should conduct himself with integrity and truthfulness. Among the women I surveyed and interviewed, honesty seemed to be one of the most commonly named positive characteristics that they remembered about their fathers.

A father who provides a model of masculinity that his daughter can look up to is respected and admired throughout his daughter's lifetime. He also sets the standard by which all other men will be judged and measured.

Conversely, men who abandon or abuse their daughters set them up for a lifetime of pain, distrust, and feelings of

Women's Comments
on Their Dads' Best Qualities

- Consistency and love.
- Provision—a strong work ethic.
- Honest, hardworking, reliable, trustworthy.
- The spirit of giving. He gave to so many people and touched so many lives.
- He was reliable, honest, a hard worker, smart, and an excellent provider.
- Dad's best character trait is his integrity and honesty.
- Honesty—I don't think my father ever said something that he didn't believe was true. He expected the same from others.
- He is a lifelong learner and is very tenacious.
- My dad has a strong work ethic.
- Compassion.
- Honesty—he was the most honest person I have ever known.
- Strength, work ethic, and sense of humor.

worthlessness. You can feel the pain in this woman's statement: "I have expectations of being special, loved, cared for, and protected that my spouse is not able to live up to. I grew up feeling angry, unloved, unappreciated, not accepted. I knew my value, but I struggle with believing that others know my value, even God."

When men are angry or disrespectful to the females in their families, it sets their daughters up to expect this kind of treatment from men. If a man does not provide for and protect his family, his daughters have no expectations of this behavior from the men they enter into relationships with. Why would a woman willingly marry a man who can't or won't hold a job to support his family? Why would she intentionally marry a man who abuses her? Probably, she wouldn't choose to do so intentionally. Perhaps that was the type of man who was modeled for her growing up and she is subconsciously attracted to that model, believing she deserves that kind of treatment and is unworthy of anything better.

One woman summed up the power of a positive male role model this way: "I'm not married but I do know that I had a great example of a husband because I think the greatest influence my dad had on me is how he treated my mother. He loved her and honored her and protected her."

The Effects of Fatherlessness on Women

What happens when Dad isn't in his daughter's life? Does he still influence how she relates to men? Remember that a man does not have to be physically absent for a girl to be fatherless. He can also be emotionally, spiritually, and psychologically absent (or abusive) and still wreak the same havoc in his daughter's life by his noninvolvement.

"A common theme among women who did not have a father is the inability to trust a man and to believe that he won't go away. Counting on and loving a man is a leap of faith, because for them a permanent relationship with a man is entirely theoretical. These women tend to test the men in their lives by starting fights, finding flaws, or expecting to be abandoned."[4]

One woman who grew up fatherless readily admitted to me that she spent many years pushing her husband as far as she could just to test him and make sure he wouldn't leave her. Her fear of abandonment nearly drove her marriage into a self-fulfilling prophecy.

Fatherless girls also tend to idealize their absent fathers. Women who fall into the trap of comparing their husbands

Women's Comments
on Their Dads' Worst Qualities

- Controlling toward Mom and us kids.
- Anger and manipulation.
- He was reactive in disciplinary situations—didn't really have room for gray areas.
- Emotional abandonment. I felt like he wished I'd never been born, often he just told me to go away, or drove me away by his harshness. He lectured to us, but never talked with us.
- Selfishness.
- Not being willing to stand up for himself or those that God put in his care.
- He was not there to protect, nurture, or support his children.
- He tends to pick on people and put people down. He seems to think he is teasing, but I always felt instead of being praised for a job well done he would say, "Why didn't you do better?" He was also very authoritative. He was definitely the boss and there was no questioning any decision he made. Even now if I have an opinion different than his, he considers me to be wrong and will tell me I should have the same opinion that he does.
- Mean.
- An impatient anger—he was easily frustrated. He was in no way abusive in his anger or impatience but he modeled an angry tone of voice, angry facial expressions, and angry body language.
- He talked "at" us, and not with us. He demanded respect but didn't give any.

and boyfriends to the ideal image they have created of an absent father are always disappointed—not because the men are inadequate, but because the women have distorted images of fathers and men. Likewise, women with absent or poor role models for fathers are often more loyal toward them than those with positive role models. For instance, women with abusive fathers or fathers in prison tend to idealize them and overlook their many faults, even replacing those faults with fictionalized accounts of their good deeds and positive attributes. The parent who is absent always has the advantage of never being found imperfect. Fatherless girls tend to imagine good and valid reasons why their fathers have abandoned them rather than face the devastating fact that they might not love them. They project sterling qualities upon them and imagine romantic notions as to why their fathers are not interested in them. They then make excuses for them long after being proven wrong.

Another common trait among these abandoned women is an anxiety about being dependent upon a man and not being able to support themselves. They have been taught that they cannot trust or depend upon a man. Other characteristics of fatherless women are sexual anxiety and the desire for older men who exhibit paternal characteristics.

Women who do not receive healthy masculine love and affection as girls from their fathers have a craving for it throughout their lives. Many women are either willing to substitute or confuse sex for love in their desire for masculine affection. As I think back when I was young, all of the girls available for sexual favors came from either fatherless or abusive backgrounds. Of course the young men did not recognize it as such then, merely as opportunity.

Daughters who have had the benefit of healthy father involvement are more independent, self-possessed, and more likely to assume responsibility for the consequences of their actions. Father-deprived girls show precocious sexual interest (they are three times more likely to become pregnant out of wedlock than their fathered counterparts) and have less ability to maintain sexual and emotional attachment with just one male. Without a father, girls must learn about boys without a man's perspective. They are like sheep without a shepherd. Without his influence and guidance, even the most normal male activities may seem bizarre and strange to her.

Angela Thomas says, "I can be in a small group of women and tell you in a matter of moments which ones have had a healthy, loving relationship with their fathers. There is a certain confidence and peace that comes from a woman who has known such love. And there is an anxiousness and insecurity buried inside a woman who has never known a father's love or, worse, who has suffered wounds from his words or his distance or his hands."[5] Women who have been hurt deeply in some way by their fathers tend to either take that pain out on men throughout their lifetimes, or become victims of men.

Without a father around to provide a role model, healthy physical affection, and protection for her, a girl is left to the examples of manhood she sees on television, the movies, and music videos—by all accounts very poor options. Fathers can act as filters for much of the "noise" our culture throws at her. Without that filter girls are stressed and bewildered. They are left to the mercy of the young men (many of whom never had fathers either) who prowl around her like packs of wolves. Males have an internal radar that can detect female sexual availability or vulnerability. This exposes young girls and women to predators who prey upon them and manipulate their unconscious desire and yearning for father-love. Combine this with their natural longing for an older male's physical and emotional affection, and we see an increase in unwed, teenage mothers, perpetuating the cycle anew. Many fatherless women fall for the first male who shows them any kind of affection or attention that they crave.

Without a model of how a woman and man interact together, a girl is left on her own to learn about the mysterious and frightening world of males—she doesn't have the real thing at home to watch and examine. One fatherless woman said, "I was fascinated by men. I wanted to please them, therefore I compromised some of my values." Another stated, "I was begging for any man to love me. I never believed anyone would love me if they knew me. I sought any attention I could from men—time, touch, promises." And still another said it this way: "I tend to be drawn to any man who pays attention to me. I feel flattered and surprised by the attention. I guess I sell myself short."

Any child deprived of his or her God-given right to a father in their lives suffers from father-hunger. Both boys and girls suffer from this father-hunger, yet each expresses it differently as adults. Says Dr. Frank Pittman,

> Women strangle their partners by trying to get the closeness they didn't get from their fathers. But men are fatherless too. They've been raised by women who had all this emotional power over them because their fathers were nowhere in sight. Most men have only known the male mythology of proving their manhood by escaping from Mom, and by having a woman respond to them sexually.
>
> So the fatherless girl and the fatherless boy are going to have quite different fantasies about what the other is supposed to do. Her fantasies have to do with wanting a wonderfully strong, nurturing man who will devote his full attention to her, because her father didn't. His fantasy is that he has to get her sexual attention to affirm his masculinity, but make sure she doesn't get control of him emotionally, because his father wasn't around to show him another way to be a man.[6]

Any woman, but especially a fatherless one, can benefit greatly from understanding and recognizing the influences her father had in her life and the choices she makes, as well as from exploring the background and paternal legacy of the man she's interested in as well.

A Father's Influence on a Woman's Choices

> Women's childhood relationships with their fathers are important to them all their lives. Regardless of age or status, women who seem clearest about their goals and most satisfied with their lives and personal and family relationships usually remember that their fathers enjoyed them and were actively interested in their development.
>
> Stella Chess and Jane Whitbread, *Daughters*

In what ways does a father influence the choices his daughter makes in life, especially in her relationships? One area in which a woman's father plays a major role is the sexual decision-making process of a woman. For instance, girls with uninvolved or absent fathers tend to become sexually active at an earlier age than their fathered peers.

Victoria Secunda in her book *Women and Their Fathers: The Sexual and Romantic Impact of the First Man in Your Life* (as the father of a daughter, I find the title to be a little creepy), states this about a father's influence:

> The father-daughter relationship is the proving ground for a daughter's romantic attachments, her dress rehearsal for heterosexual love. Numerous studies point to the fact that a woman's capacity for a mutually loving and sexually fulfilling attachment is *directly* related to her relationship to her father.

129

> *And women who have difficulties in this area almost always*
> *had fathers who could not be counted on, or who were emotion-*
> *ally or physically unavailable, when they were growing up.*[7]

A woman's father also plays a significant role in her relation-ship choices, either consciously or unconsciously. A woman with a positive relationship with her dad may tend to gravitate toward men who have the same characteristics. A woman who resents or despises her father may look for a man with the op-posite qualities, or unconsciously marry a man with similar qualities and resent him. This can cause much confusion if a woman is not attuned to these influences.

Women who have not had a model of healthy masculinity in their lives often have trouble detecting predators, abusers, and men who will abandon them. They are in some ways like a lamb left to the wolves. Oftentimes, these women continue to choose the same "type" of men, getting the same results over and over again. In contrast, women who have had a good man in their lives have had a model by which to judge men.

The community I live in has two megachurches. The first was founded by two extremely gifted and powerful men who have positively impacted and changed the lives of thou-sands of people, including my own. One of the founders left the pulpit several years ago and has gone on to be a very successful author of both Christian fiction and nonfiction, although he is still very active in the church. When the re-maining founder decided to retire, a search was conducted for his replacement. It was decided that the son-in-law of the founder who had initially left the pulpit would be groomed for the position.

The other church was grown by a dynamic pastor over the past twenty years from a small dying congregation to one of over 20,000 members. As this man is now seeking to move on in life, the young pastor selected to replace him is, no surprise, his son-in-law as well.

At first glance, many people might think nepotism or favoritism is involved in these choices. However, both of these young men are very talented and gifted pastors. It got me thinking: is it just coincidence, or did these powerful leaders both produce daughters who unconsciously sought out men with as much potential to be great men as their fathers?

A woman's father is the biggest influence in the way she relates to men. If you can understand the influence and role your father played in your life, it can dramatically help you recognize how and why you use your influence. It also explains much about the kind of man you are attracted to and why—and possibly why a woman might feel a need to "change" her man.

I encourage you to spend some time thinking about your relationship with your father and your current relationship with the man in your life. Then spend some time in conversation with your heavenly Father. You might need to ask him to help you forgive your earthly father. Or you may need to ask him to heal some wounds or to help clarify and understand some areas that are confusing to you. Be open to what God is telling you about yourself, your father, your husband, and your relationship as a daughter to your heavenly Father. Ask him for discernment in knowing how to best use your power of influence for the good of the men in your life.

8

Sex Is *Not* a Weapon

Being a sex symbol has to do with an attitude, not looks. Most men think it's looks, most women know otherwise.

Kathleen Turner, quoted in the *London Observer*

A woman's sexuality may be the most powerful influence factor she has going for her with regard to her man. A woman's strong persuasion in this area can be used to help change, grow, and improve not only her man's life but hers as well.

How Men View Sex

Like just about everything else in life, men and women tend to view sex differently. Higher levels of the hormone testosterone and its effects on the male body and psyche create a much higher sex drive in men than women. God created men like this to perpetuate the species. I tell my wife whenever she fends off my advances that I'm just trying to obey God's command to replenish the earth.

Men view romance as a prelude to sex. Romance for a woman serves to make her feel honored, cherished, and loved. My wife says that being romanced makes her feel like the apple of my eye—the way we all want to believe God feels about us. Women are wired to feel fulfilled by nonsexual affection. When they receive it, they naturally respond with physical affection. Men are wired to feel fulfilled with sexual affection. It is a man's responsibility in God's order to first serve a woman by honoring and cherishing her with nonsexual affection in order to ultimately get his physical needs met.

Unfortunately, many men get that turned around. In their desire to get their own needs met, they neglect to fulfill their woman's needs first. God wired them with this drive to procreate, yet the world has twisted that desire into lust.

At the risk of perpetuating a stereotype about men, there's a distinct possibility that if women knew what men really think about, they would refuse to be in the same room with us. They'd think us perverted. Guys think about sex all the time—even in the most inappropriate places such as in church or at funerals.

Males can be stimulated by nothing—for no reason at all. They can become aroused purely as a physical function of their gender. "The human male, because of sperm production and other factors, naturally desires sexual release about every forty-eight to seventy-two hours."[1] That's every two to three days! My wife accuses me of having made up this statistic.

That males think about sex a lot may not be press-stopping news to some of you, but the depth of how it impacts their everyday lives might come as a surprise.

Men reportedly think about sex an average of thirty-three times per day, or twice an hour. Some people say women only think about sex once a day . . . when men ask for it.[2] You can imagine how distracting sex can be for males when they spend so much time and energy thinking about it.

Even subconsciously, men are always aware of the women around them. In fact, because God created him that way, I think it is probably impossible for a man not to notice a female body. For instance, you can have a whole room full of men and only one woman (especially if she's physically attractive) and every man in the room will be conscious of where she is at every moment. In addition, they will all act much differently than they would if she were not present. It's one of the reasons we do not allow women inside the room when presenting workshops to men—it prohibits the guys from being open, honest, and vulnerable. A woman's mere presence changes the entire dynamics of the room. Even the scent of a woman can alter a man's attitude and bearing.

How to Motivate Him

Men can be motivated in a variety of ways—the most powerful being respect and admiration. But as any woman knows, men are often motivated by one of two other desires as well—one being food, the other being the area a little below their stomachs.

After the birth of our two children, my wife, Suzanne, felt it was healthier for her to remain off the pill. But having to rely on alternative forms of birth control was putting a cramp on the spontaneity of our sex life. To solve this problem, Suzanne came up with what she considered a brilliant solution. The only trouble was, I wasn't too thrilled about the words "cold, sharp steel" mentioned in the same sentence with that part of my anatomy. So while she was trying to convince me to have a vasectomy, she used one of the most logical motivations she could think of. She earnestly reasoned with me that once I had this "simple little operation" we would be able to have "fun" any*time* and any*where* I wanted. Like an ox being led to slaughter, I readily complied.

The day of the procedure, I must have looked like a terrified, trembling stallion with the whites of my eyes flashing. The only thing I remember about that fateful day was that all the nurses kept a close eye on me and even stationed a nurse between me and the door, as if I might bolt at any moment. I was sorely tempted.

Of course, much to my chagrin, Suzanne's enticement ended up not being entirely true, but it certainly motivated me to overcome my trepidation of having the procedure performed. My point is that sex means a lot to a man. Males consider sex one of the basic needs in life—right up there with air, food, and water. Meeting his physical needs is imperative to a successful marriage.

Keep in mind, though, that a man would rather have less sex with a willing partner than more sex with a woman who considers it a "duty." So, if his partner has the attitude of "Okay, let's get it over with," he might not turn it down, but it will not be very satisfying to him. When you desire him physically, you have the power to salve many of the wounds this world inflicts upon him. *A man who is desired by his wife meets the world with confidence and enthusiasm.*

God designed sex to play an important role in a marriage relationship. "Let the husband render to his wife the affection due her, and likewise also the wife to her husband. The wife does not have authority over her own body, but the husband does. And likewise the husband does not have authority over his own body, but the wife does. Do not deprive one another except with consent for a time, that you may give yourselves to fasting and prayer; and come together again so that Satan does not tempt you because of your lack of self-control" (1 Cor. 7:3–5 NKJV).

This passage speaks frankly to the fact that married couples should have normal, healthy sexual relations—that depriving either partner of their natural rights in this area may be conducive to temptation or sexual immorality. Both husband and wife have conjugal privileges and exclusive possession of the other in this area.

While sex is a powerful *physical* need for a man, it is much more than that. Sex also fulfills a powerful *emotional* need for your husband. Author and columnist Shaunti Feldhahn provides this analogy: "Lack of sex is as emotionally serious to him as, say, his sudden silence would be to you, were he simply to stop communicating with you. It is just as wounding to him, just as much a legitimate grievance—and just as dangerous to your marriage."[3]

Feldhahn continues: "In a very deep way, your man often feels isolated and burdened by secret feelings of inadequacy. Making love with you assures him that you find him desirable, salves a deep sense of loneliness, and gives him the strength and well-being necessary to face the world with confidence. And, of course, sex also makes him feel loved—in fact, he can't feel completely loved without it."[4]

If you want your husband to respond romantically, you have to put him ahead of your children. Yes, your children are important, but your husband is more important. Make him a priority. Your marriage is the foundation that your children are raised upon. Many men feel they take a backseat to their children in the eyes of their wives. By putting your husband's needs first, you are modeling a good example for your children to follow. You are also inspiring him to be more amenable to romance.

A truly wonderful thing I've noticed over the years is that my wife becomes exceptionally beautiful and attractive whenever she compliments me. Every time she tells me how dashing and handsome I am, she just sparkles with beauty. I'm not sure which universal law of dynamics applies to this circumstance, but it works every time.

So what things are important to him in this area? First of all, don't be afraid to try new things in the bedroom (or any other room, for that matter). Your willingness to initiate things once in a while provides a novel boost to him. Men typically don't have affairs because of lust, but due to boredom—they seek adventure in their lives. I've read other books that suggested occasionally meeting your husband at the door with no clothes on when he comes home from work. I won't say whether I've ever had that experience before, but it sure sounds like a positive motivational activity to me.

If you can give him a little adventure occasionally, he'll be content to "sow his own fields," so to speak.

When a man feels that his wife desires him, it gives him a big boost of self-confidence. Believe me, if a man has a wife at home who respects him, believes in him, and desires him, he won't be looking for anything else outside his home.

One of the most basic needs of a man is that he desires to feel wanted physically by a woman. If he doesn't feel wanted by his wife, he may look to satisfy that strong need elsewhere.

His need for you physically is one of the most influential areas a wife has. Used properly, it can be not only fun and uplifting but extremely motivating as well.

Why Men Won't Commit

For those of you who are single and have not had sex with your man—whether by choice or by circumstance—there may be numerous reasons why he won't commit to the next step. But be warned that having sex with him will not give you what you hope for.

For those of you who are single and are sleeping with your man, and you're wondering why he won't commit to the next step in the relationship, consider how men view sex. This is how most men feel about sex and relationships: "Why buy the cow when you're getting the milk for free?" No, I'm not equating women to cows—that's why it's called an analogy. I'm not trying to disparage women, but I am pointing out that men are perfectly willing to take anything they can get without having to work for it.

There is a big difference between sex and love. Most men know the difference. Do you?

According to the National Marriage Project at Rutgers University, the number one reason men don't commit is that they know they can get sex without getting married.[5] Even though the sexual revolution created and endorsed a cafeteria selection of intimate arrangements for women, it appears that men reap the benefits in most of these situations, especially cohabitation. Living together is nearly considered par for the course today. Many young people believe that they cannot determine whether their companion would be compatible in marriage without "testing the waters," so to speak, by living together. This assumption is false for a variety of reasons, the most damaging being because living together allows young men to reap all the benefits of marriage without any of the obligations. These men get their laundry done, their meals cooked, and all the sex they want. If things do not turn out to their satisfaction, they can just pack up and find a better living arrangement.

While women invest themselves into these relationships (maybe deeper than they realize), men get a good deal without the risk of financial devastation from divorce. Oftentimes she is expecting an intimate relationship to gradually deepen, eventually culminating in marriage. He, on the other hand, considers the arrangement a nonpermanent situation. Since he isn't married, he has no moral obligation if a better deal comes along.

A new study shows that fewer cohabiting couples actually end up marrying each other than previously believed. Only about 40 percent of women who cohabitate actually get married to the man they are living with.[6]

While cohabitation is certainly a more convenient situation for all parties involved, women usually risk the most in these situations. Women who avoid getting prematurely enmeshed in a relationship have an opportunity to learn about a man's character, conduct, and intentions without the risk of wasting their valuable time and money and the heartbreak of the dissolution of the relationship.

Marriage-minded women should understand that they cannot casually give away their most valuable commodity—sex. Not when it can be used as a source of power and advantage. I understand that sounds rather callous, but women have either lost the realization of the true value of their bodies, or they just don't care anymore.

If you are in a sexual relationship with a man and wonder why the man in your life won't commit to marriage or an exclusive relationship, think about the things that motivate nearly all men. What would be a man's motivation to marry a woman, especially one who's had children with another man? Single men are generally only motivated by things that serve their own self-interests, or to satisfy their basic needs. Occasionally, some men will rise above themselves and put their families, and maybe even the community, before themselves, but it's generally rare. I don't think this is intentional or even selfish in most cases; it's just the way guys look at life.

For those of you who are not having sex and agonize over the question, "If I break down and have sex, then will he commit to me?" the answer is probably not. If you do break down and have sex in hopes he will commit, you might get what you are hoping for, but more than likely it will be your worst nightmare. How many women have kicked themselves the next morning, saying, "I knew I shouldn't have done it, but I did anyway. I can't believe I was so stupid."

If sex isn't the number one item on most men's self-gratification list, it's not very far down. Typically, most men are pretty satisfied as long as they have a dry place to sleep, have food in their bellies, and are getting their sexual needs met on at least a semiregular basis. Immature men are usually *only* looking for a warm bed and a woman to make them feel like a man. Why would any normal, healthy (key word *healthy*) man commit to all the problems and stresses associated with marriage if he is having *all* his basic needs met? My point is that if you live with a man outside of marriage or give him all the sex he could want, what is his motivation to get married? I know that many people in our culture will consider that to be an archaic, prudish, or unenlightened attitude. But again, just because it goes against what the majority of people may believe or want to believe does not mean it isn't true.

Think about this—if you engage in sexual intimacy with a man without the commitment of marriage, he knows at least one important thing about you—he knows he doesn't have to work very hard to get you or to keep you. When you allow yourself to be used to satisfy his sexual urges, you lose all power and any control in the relationship. It's really a matter of respect—and men value respect highly. They don't esteem a woman who doesn't respect herself any more than to give herself away cheaply. "Once they have casual sex, men say, they are less respectful and interested in pursuing a relationship with a woman."[7] Men who are willing to settle for a woman like this generally end up being no big prize themselves.

If you think I'm being unduly harsh on men, just remember how many dates most men are generally willing to take you on before expecting sex in return. If they don't get "repaid" within the first couple of dates, they will probably hit the road in search of greener, or at least easier, pastures to plow.

Women tend to romanticize sex. But to men premarital sex is just that—sex. They compartmentalize it to be just a physical function or need that is enjoyable. Yes, it's better with someone a man loves, but it's good all the time anyway. In fact for some men it might even be more exciting without being all clouded up and entangled with a relationship.

However, understand that even though this might seem hypocritical, few men want to marry a woman who has slept around with a lot of other men. Most men still want to marry a woman they are comfortable will pass inspection when bringing her home to mom and dad. Men, probably even more than women, hate to think of the woman they marry having slept with another man—it's intrinsically very threatening to his manhood. It's why the ultimate "get even" or revenge a woman can extract on a man is to have sex with either his best friend or his worst enemy. It is devastating to his ego. Perhaps it is also because men intrinsically know that women should place more value on their bodies than to give them away frivolously or use them as a weapon of destruction and pain.

Also, understand that the *type* of men you choose to be with will probably determine the quality of men you will be able to attract in the future. For instance, if you think you will be able to sleep around with men of low character and then find a nice guy to marry, you might be in for a surprise. Most men have standards that say if a woman has "been" with a certain type of man, they do not consider that woman worthy of marrying. Some women have rued a mistake they made early on for the rest of their lives by being limited in the kind of man who was willing to marry them.

Men view sex in a completely different light than women do. Women are often seeking intimacy in relationships. Men are more apt to be able to enjoy casual sex whether they have feelings for a woman or not. Hence, women are willing to trade sex for intimacy, while men will give intimacy in order to get sex. However, it doesn't mean that they are really in love with a woman. In other words, a male will often say or do anything if he thinks it will get him what he wants in terms of sex. Intellectually, most women know this, yet they continue to trade what should be their most valuable asset for the illusion of love. A woman's body (and especially her virginity) is an exquisite gift to her husband from her and God. If it has been valued by her and not abused, it is a treasure that he will appreciate his entire life. If a woman treasures her body, it will make it much more valuable in a man's eyes. But if she does not value her body, giving it away freely and often, a man will probably not prize that gift either.

Many men understand that giving a woman the affection she craves leads to sex. They learn how to talk to a woman, be interested in her needs and desires, pay attention to her, and shower her with gifts, flowers, and nonsexual affection. Many women see this in a man and capitulate by responding sexually (which is natural—it's what she responds to), only to find out that they were used. In fact, frequently a woman is swept off her feet by a caring and responsive man during courtship, only to find the communication and affection stops once he gets what he wants. Oftentimes men look at affection as a means to an end, while women view it as a necessary component to a relationship.

Lust

Lust in a man has nothing to do with you whatsoever as his wife or girlfriend. It is not about you! It is an issue that a man struggles with, within himself. It is a battle between the factions of his soul. It is not due to anything you do or don't do, nor the way you look, how much you weigh, or how adept you are at satisfying him sexually. All men struggle with lust to one degree or another. Even men who are married to Victoria's Secret models lust for other women. A man learns to control this impulse partly as a function of the amount of respect he has for a woman, but it still lurks in the background of his consciousness. It is unrealistic to think that a man will never struggle with this issue in his heart regardless of how much he loves you.

Once you remove yourself from that equation and understand that it has nothing to do with you, you can begin to help him deal with this masculine bane in a more effective and productive manner.

Probably the best way you can help him deal with issues of lust is to hold him accountable for his actions (such as not viewing pornography) and then use some creativity in initiating an adventurous sexuality from time to time.

The fact is, nearly all men are addicted to sex. We compulsively look to women for gratification. I know that not everyone will agree with this statement, but that is why I have a hard time believing sexual addiction is anything other than a loss of self-control and self-restraint. Yes, I know that exposure to pornography releases chemicals in the brain in men similar to cocaine in their addiction capabilities, creating the same kind of "high" and craving for more. But I also know the same struggles that I (and nearly every man I know) have with controlling my own lustful nature. And I also recognize that if I allowed myself, I too could become a sexual addict, as could any man.

The problem with any deep-seated craving (as men have for sex) is that when we indulge it illicitly, we are only temporarily satisfied. Like any addiction, our appetite for it returns with a vengeance. The craving never ends, with the fix needed to achieve the same "high" always becoming greater. That is why men who do not use self-restraint (such as with a sexual addiction), even when having sex with many different women, are never anything but miserable.

A woman who understands and appreciates her sexuality has a tremendous advantage in using this powerful tool to influence the life of her husband. Like any powerful mechanism, though, it must be treated with respect. Because it fulfills such a robust need in her man, it can be used as a weapon if not used properly. Learn as much about it as you can so that it can be used positively to encourage and inspire your man to be all he's capable of.

9

The Top Ten Things about Men That Drive Women Crazy

If a man speaks in the forest and there is no woman around to hear him, is he still wrong?

Bumper sticker

For those of you who looked at the table of contents and came straight to this chapter hoping to find out how to "fix" your man, welcome. But I hope you'll go back and read the other chapters when you have time.

In a daring exhibition of courage, I encouraged all the women on my rather large email database to send me their Top Ten Things about Men That Drive Women Crazy. Needless to say, I received a *lot* of replies. As I read through them, I had to laugh because, other than those that were mean-spirited, almost all of them were true! I was amused because (1) the women were so eager and excited to get these grievances off their chests, and (2) because I knew they were true (I recognized most of them in myself). So, let me just list the ten most popular and I will give you my feedback and insights into the male psyche for each one. Perhaps that will help you understand and recognize that you are not alone out there.

Let me say one thing, though, to keep in mind before we get started. I'd like you to truly think about a statement I'm going to make. When you first read it, your natural inclination will be to automatically disregard it. If a woman told you this, you would nod your head sagely and think she made a profound point. When I say it, you will be tempted to dismiss me as a male chauvinist pig. Here goes: *It takes a lot less effort to make a man happy and contented than it does a woman.*

Think about this for a minute, because it is important to get the proper perspective before continuing. Given a man and a woman who are normal and healthy, I think you will agree that I am correct—men are lower maintenance than females. This is important because if you judge men on the same scale you do women, you'll be continually disappointed and let down. *You can't expect a man to be a man and then get mad at him for not acting more like a woman.* But if you recognize that a relationship with a man, while different, takes less effort than, say, a friendship with your girlfriend, you'll be pleased and have lower expectations.

Also, women tend to experience more anger in their relationships than men do. They generally are angry at their mate more often and for longer periods than men. It tends to take a woman longer to process her anger than it does her spouse.

Men typically blow off their anger and then get over it more quickly. For the most part, what a man wants most from his relationship and home is tranquility. He wants the house clean, the children well-behaved, appliances in working order, and a happy wife—a place where he can come home to recharge and relax. If he comes home to an angry wife, his frustration is in not knowing how to satisfy her needs.

My wife tells women that it will be easier to get their needs met when their husband's needs are met. When both partners are needy, they do not have the emotional reserves to give to the other to meet their needs. Since a man is generally the simpler and more easily satisfied creature, it makes sense that if a woman wants her needs met, she has to satisfy those of her man first. Someone needs to go first. I understand that women are already burdened with most of the nurturing responsibilities in a relationship, but it may be a simple fact of life. And recognizing it may help end much of the frustration you are experiencing in your relationship.

So, in the spirit of fun, here are the most-cited Top Ten Things about Men That Drive Women Crazy, in no particular order.

He Doesn't Help with Housework

I was bombarded with comments like, "Men go to work, come home, and think their day is done. A woman's day is *never* done." Another comment that fit nicely in this category was "Men are unaware of the messes they make. They also either pretend not to know, or are not sure of the definition of 'clean.'"

Men do seem to have a proclivity to be able to step over dirty clothes on the floor or ignore dirty dishes in the sink. And their definition of clean is probably a little more lax than most women's. It's also true that most men do not help out with the housework as much as they could or probably should. But we are getting better.

According to a recent study, husbands currently shoulder about 40 percent of the household chore load.[1]

Also, there may be good reasons why men are more comfortable working outside of the home—it's safer. A recent study by the American Heart Association found that men who considered themselves househusbands had an 82 percent higher death rate compared to their counterparts who worked outside the home.[2]

This woman summed up many women's feelings about this issue rather well with the following comments:

> Women want men who are protectors and contribute in the traditional "manly" ways, but in our society today, it's as if women have to be everything a man is plus take on her traditional female duties. I have to take care of the yard, get the cars in for maintenance, do all the scheduling for doctors, teachers, do the laundry, arrange for home repairs. . . . What on earth does he do besides go to a job during the day? I work all day at a job AND try to do all the rest of these things—he comes home and does nothing in comparison!

Another put it more succinctly: "He sits around the television during all his free time."

I watched a show on television the other night about a primitive native tribe that lives along the Amazon River. When interviewed through a translator, the women of the tribe complained that all the men did was go hunting and then come home and sit around staring at the campfire. Sounds like some things are the same all over the world, doesn't it?

WINTER CLASSES FOR MEN AT THE LEARNING CENTER FOR ADULTS

NOTE: DUE TO THE COMPLEXITY AND DIFFICULTY LEVEL OF THEIR CONTENTS, CLASS SIZES WILL BE LIMITED TO 8 PARTICIPANTS MAXIMUM.

The Toilet Paper Roll—Does It Change Itself?
Round Table Discussion. Meets 2 weeks, Saturday 12:00 for 2 hours.

Is It Possible to Urinate Using the Technique of Lifting the Seat and Avoiding the Floor, Walls, and Nearby Bathtub?
Group Practice Meets 4 weeks, Saturday 10:00 PM for 2 hours.

Learning How to Find Things—Starting with Looking in the Right Places and Not Turning the House Upside Down While Screaming
Open Forum. Monday at 8:00 PM, 2 hours.

Real Men Ask for Directions When Lost—Real-Life Testimonials
Tuesdays at 6:00 PM, location to be determined.

Learning to Live—Basic Differences Between Mother and Wife
Online Classes and role-playing. Tuesdays at 7:00 PM, location to be determined.

How to Be the Ideal Shopping Companion
Relaxation Exercises, Meditation, and Breathing Techniques. Meets 4 weeks, Tuesday and Thursday for 2 hours beginning at 7:00 PM.

The Stove/Oven—What It Is and How It Is Used
Live Demonstration. Tuesdays at 6:00 PM, location to be determined.

Excerpted from anonymous email

I don't have any brilliant insight into the minds of men on why they don't do more housework other than ... we just don't want to. But perhaps there are ways that men could be motivated to help out with the housework that would produce better results than nagging.

One woman said, "To most women, it is *very* romantic to have our husbands helping around the house and with the kids. It's true, you know—sex begins in the kitchen."

I don't know if that's true or not, but I can assure you that many men are not aware of this fact. It wouldn't hurt to let him know if you feel that way. I'm pretty sure if most guys knew that by doing a load of laundry or washing the dishes every so often they would significantly increase their likelihood of getting "lucky," you can bet they'd be a lot more motivated to do housework without being reminded.

He Shuts Down Emotionally

Several dozen women commented that men were either unwilling or unable to share their feelings and talk about their problems. They felt if a man needed time to sort things through, he should say so and make a commitment to talk about the issue within a reasonable length of time.

Recognizing, understanding, and dealing with emotions are difficult for men. Men express their emotions differently than women. For example, a man will *do* things for a woman to show her he cares. He tells her he loves her by washing her car or changing the oil in it. I always make sure I regularly check all the fluids, tires, and operating conditions of my wife's car for her. Doing things for you is a man's language of love.

Part of the problem men have with emotions is fear—men don't understand emotions and thus cannot control them. Not being in control of something as powerful as emotions is pretty scary to a guy. The other part is that men are raised to not nurture our emotional side. Boys are brought up to be tough, resilient, and self-sufficient. Part of the process mandates that they learn to hide both physical and emotional pain. Boys aren't expected to cry as much as girls, and they are often not nurtured to recognize and understand their emotions as much as girls. Maybe because boys are slower to develop verbal skills than girls, we do not talk as much or as deeply as women do. Perhaps because men are so physical, we just assume males are as tough on the inside as on the outside.

Boys then, ashamed of being vulnerable, learn to suffer in silence and to mask their emotions. A boy learns early in life that to show pain or fear or vulnerability is to invite a deluge of criticism, taunting, and teasing from his peers. The unwritten "code" of boys teaches him that he must keep his needs, his loneliness, his powerlessness, and his fears inside—to never complain or cry about his hardships or problems. Boys learn to hide their suffering behind a mask of stoicism or, worse, one of anger. They "learn to wear the mask so skillfully . . . they don't even know they are doing it."[3]

Unfortunately, this masking of emotions prevents them from learning who they really are. Especially for those of us who endured traumatic childhoods, the protective husk we hide our soft and vulnerable underbelly with also serves to keep our emotions frozen.

I can remember being proud of the fact that I never shed a tear as an adult man for approximately twenty years. The truth is, my emotions were frozen. I couldn't feel anything (except anger) because I had covered my emotions so well as a protective defense mechanism. Once God began healing my internal wounds, it was like he melted my frozen heart. Now I'm an old softy—I end up blubbering at the drop of a hat. I guess that liquid from my melting heart has to go somewhere.

Many of the emotional trials that all boys are forced to endure produce traits and skills that are necessary to survive and succeed as men. Unfortunately, boys who are guarded too closely by overprotective mothers seldom earn (through life's hard knocks) the toughened character necessary to be a full and complete man—a man capable of defending, protecting, and providing for a family. But without the proper guidance, these trials can be twisted into torturous ordeals with devastating consequences. At best, some of these trials and initiations strengthen a boy into the hardened oak he needs to be to lead a family. At worst, they cripple him emotionally.

That's why men shut down emotionally.

So, how can a woman use her influence to help a man be more in touch with his emotions? As silly as it sounds, one simple thing that helped me was one of those charts that shows all the different faces with the names of the emotions beneath them. My wife told me she put it on our refrigerator door to help our son recognize what he was feeling, but I'm a little suspicious that it was directed toward me as well. Nonetheless, that kind of visual feedback can help a man recognize what he is feeling.

He Doesn't Listen or Remember

Many of my email correspondents spoke about men having "selective" listening and attested to their poor or complete lack of communication skills. Additionally, the point was made abundantly clear that men have a tendency to offer solutions for problems before they understand the whole issue, and that they are always trying to "fix" rather than listen.

"Guilty as charged." Men do have trouble listening and do try to fix problems. But perhaps some of it is the way the message is delivered. Remember that if you don't get to the point right away, men's minds drift quickly.

I think men do listen; we just don't always hear what women say. Sometimes we are preoccupied. Sometimes it has to do with the ways our minds work—that constant "seek and destroy" program that looks for problems to fix. We listen selectively because we are only looking for the problem and thinking about the solution. All the other stuff is just noise. Frankly, it is difficult sometimes wading through all the details that women work into everyday conversation. Those just don't seem relevant to the point at hand.

Also, just because a man does not make eye contact doesn't mean he isn't listening. Most men cannot process what's being said to them if they make eye contact for longer than a couple of seconds without looking away.

Communication and relationships expert John Gray says, "When a man listens, his basic tendency is to look away in order to think about what is being said. . . . If a man simply stares into a woman's eyes when she talks about feelings, his mind will start to go blank and he will space out."[4]

Along the same lines, another oft-repeated point involved men's poor memories, which is probably linked to poor listening skills (at least, many women think so). I am assuming the complaint about a man's lack of memory has to do with things like remembering his wife's birthday, their wedding anniversary, what she wore on their first date, picking up the kids from school, and so on. Do men have poor memories? Probably—although I don't have any trouble remembering sports statistics. I also don't have a problem remembering to regularly change the oil in the car. And every red-blooded American male over the age of forty-five can remember where he was when Carlton Fisk hit the winning home run in game six of the 1975 World Series against the Cincinnati Reds. So maybe men's memory problems just stem from stuff that doesn't interest them that much.

So, if remembering certain things is important to you, here's how you might help your husband. Create anticipation. While I know that women think that by men remembering anniversaries and birthdays it means they love them more, men are more action oriented. Maybe good-naturedly challenging him (multiple times) to try to remember an upcoming anniversary would create a sense of competition that he would love. Be sure to make the stakes something that will motivate him to place a high priority on succeeding.

Twice in twenty-six years of marriage, my wife has made me her world-famous rigatoni. She cooks the shells and then hand-stuffs them with a delicious combination of Italian sausage, seasoned ground beef, spinach, and three types of cheeses. Then she pours her special-recipe homemade red sauce (simmered all day) and shredded cheeses over the top before baking to a golden brown and serves with garlic bread. Heck, I'd remember hers *and* all her friends' birthdays and anniversaries for a crack at her homemade rigatoni. That's motivation and anticipation! Of course, I'm an "old guy" now, so food may have moved up to the number one motivational tool for me in recent years.

He's Inconsiderate and Selfish

Hands down, this was the biggest area that women said bugged them about men. Comments like, "Inconsiderate—needs to be asked, oftentimes more than once, to do something" or "Selfish—has a need to be first" or "Not thinking about others in a given situation" or "Planning something and not thinking about all the work it takes to make it happen—especially when he is counting on me to do it" or "Not taking responsibility for his actions or words" flooded my email inbox.

Perhaps the funniest (and truest) comment I received was "Men will take the 'lazy way' if given .00001 percent the option."

In our defense I suspect this is programmed in our DNA from eons of having to conserve our energy when we were not hunting. To fail at hunting was to starve to death, and so it was important to conserve your energy to ensure success in hunting and to battle predators in the event of an attack. If you were exhausted from chopping wood, picking berries, or sweeping the cave, you might miss the opportunity to kill dinner, or be too tired to protect your family from a bear attack. So we're not really lazy; we're just conserving energy until it's needed. If you don't buy that, well, at least it sounds reasonable.

Yes, men can be lazy. And all of us will allow (or even encourage) a woman to do something for us if she is willing. Blame our mothers. Her willingness to do for her son is how he develops that mentality. Think about that with your own son.

Sometimes when men are inconsiderate, it is not intentional. I know from experience that women are often more sensitive about things, especially something spoken in conversation or an offhanded remark. Men are often preoccupied with thoughts of other things and just don't make the connection that we are being inconsiderate or insensitive. Often if you let us know why and how you thought we were being inconsiderate, we can either explain ourselves or change our behavior. Again, I think your guy wants to make you happy; he just needs to know how.

There were also plenty of comments about men not following through on commitments and promises. It's important to remember that most men do not value verbal communication as much as women do. That's again why it is important to judge a man more by his actions and not his words. But that's a whole other category . . .

He Doesn't Follow Through

Many women responded that men do not follow through on things they promised to do. The women felt like they had to keep reminding their husbands of it, making them look like "nags." Most of the complaints had to do with not completing a project or chore around the house.

I know this will sound like a lame excuse, but men forget things that are not important to them. Often what is important to you may not have as high a priority to him. It doesn't mean he didn't intend on doing it, just that it was lower on his priority list. Also, men tend to focus on one thing at a time. We do not multitask well. Thus we sometimes forget something we fully intended to do because we were distracted by something else. Each day, a man has a list of priorities to accomplish. Unfortunately, some chores often seem to slip down low on the list each day.

One area that seems to fit into this category is the phenomena of men not being able to find anything. As one woman said, "Even if it's right in front of him, he will ask me first to find it. He usually prefaces it with, 'Where did you put my . . .', as if I am spending all my spare time hiding things from him!"

I'm somewhat embarrassed to admit I suffer from this affliction. I can thoroughly rifle through a drawer or cupboard and not find what I'm searching for, no matter how hard I look. Yet my wife can walk right up and find that item instantly, often right in front of me. This seems to happen with regularity. I have to scratch my head in wonder, because my wife accuses me of not really looking, yet I know I've searched to the best of my ability. I think many men suffer from the same defect—it appears to be a male gender deficiency of some sort.

His Attitude

A number of complaints involved a man's attitude. Women accused men of always assuming the worst in any situation, and of having trouble admitting when they were wrong and apologizing (although you'd think we'd be good at it as much as we have to do it). They also felt men needed to be in control and often lacked humility.

Most of us men do struggle to admit when we are wrong. Perhaps because we are expected to be right, it creates a fear of failure within us. To be wrong is to appear weak. Nearly all men show the world a false front or cover. It's a form of protection we learn early in life. The face we show the world and how we really feel inside are rarely the same. Despite our tough-guy exterior, this façade of control and being in charge (never being wrong) often protects a vulnerable heart and ego. Men use this façade because secretly most of us men feel inadequate. We feel like imposters faking our way through life. Especially if we have not been trained and shown the way by a competent older male, we never feel confident that we can handle all the expectations life throws at us. And yet our families and the world often expect us to be perfect and to never make mistakes.

Once a man is married, this façade will be lifted now and again by one of two reasons. He will voluntarily lift it if he learns to trust his wife enough, or it will be involuntarily pushed aside when his character is such that the cover cannot continue to hold back his flaws. Men who use this false cover to hide their flaws and not just to protect their vulnerabilities will not be able to help letting their true natures show in due course. The responses of several women indicated they did not recognize that their men's false façade was hiding character flaws. These men have given them a life of heartache and despair.

His Involvement in Parenting (or Lack Thereof)

I received many comments about men being unwilling to help with discipline or to follow through with punishment. Indeed, many women felt that their husbands left the entire responsibility for the home and children on their shoulders.

One big protest was that men look at taking care of their own children as "babysitting." One woman said, "It was a given that I had to watch the kids always, including the times he was not at work. He would announce if he was going somewhere in the evening, but I was supposed to ask if he could watch the kids while I went somewhere. It's not 'babysitting' if it's your own kids."

Ouch! This one kind of hurts. My wife put a pretty firm foot down very early in our adventures in parenting that my taking care of our children was not babysitting. It seemed to be one of those nonnegotiables, so I adapted and changed my attitude. Not that I joyfully encouraged her to frequently leave me alone with the kids, but I sucked it up and took it like a man when she did. Probably the dirty little secret among men is that we know how darn hard and draining watching those little rug rats can be. We don't like to admit it to our wives, but among each other we all agree that most of the time it's a responsibility we are more than happy to hand over to our wives.

He Works Too Much

Many women objected that their men had a preoccupation with work and work-related issues, or that they put work before the family. To give this some sense of balance, I suppose working is better than the alternative. Some women have been saddled with men who do little or nothing to support their family.

Women also said that men felt the work they do outside the home is of more value and more important than what the wife does inside the home. Or if the wife works outside the home, he still considers his job more important and valuable than hers, evidenced by the wife usually being the one taking time off for sick kids, doctors' visits, and so on.

All pretty justifiable complaints, in my opinion. But, I wonder if because men feel compelled to provide for their families, they place more importance on their role. His career is an important part of his self-image. Many men I know would love to take time off during the day and take the kids to the dentist (followed by ice cream) or go to a parent/teacher conference. But the stakes of potentially losing their job is too high to jeopardize their career. Many men feel this would be irresponsible on their part. Also, even if they wouldn't admit it, I think many employers are more lenient toward women taking time from work for family issues than they would be of men.

It seems like the person who is designated as the "primary" breadwinner of the family, male or female, should be the one with fewer expectations to perform extracurricular activities away from work. It's not that each person's job is not important but that someone's job has to be *more* important in the bigger picture.

Being the primary job may not be just about money either. For instance, if your career is more secure than his with a better chance for advancement, then maybe yours is the primary career. But if your career might stop or be stalled by a pregnancy, then maybe his is more secure in the long run.

He Wants to Have Sex ALL the Time!

If you remember the chapter on sex, you know that God created men that way. Your man doesn't have a lot of choice in the matter. He really can't help it.

Look at it another way—it's pretty darn flattering that he wants you physically, even if it seems like "all the time." Along with providing for his family, sex is one of the biggest ways he expresses his love for you. It seems it would be of much more concern if he suddenly *didn't* want you anymore.

Think of this too: it is very devastating for a man to be vulnerable enough to ask for sex and then always get turned down. It would be like you begging him to speak to you and him turning a cold shoulder to you by giving you the silent treatment for months at a time. Sex helps him relieve stress, and it keeps him emotionally, psychologically, and physically healthy. It is also the best way (in his mind) you can show him you love him.

I understand that women get tired, especially when there are small children in the home. And when you are tired, you just don't feel like having sex. I also understand that some men don't recognize that you have to start the motor before you can drive the car. But I've been told (by a woman who should know) that if you go along with a good attitude even when you don't feel like it, your body will take over and you will have an enjoyable experience despite your initial low level of enthusiasm.

Women ask me during seminars with exasperation if it ever gets better—if this drive ever diminishes in men. I tell them not so far as I've experienced (to which they just shake their heads resignedly). Studies show, however, that a woman's sex drive will often increase as she gets into her mid- to late-thirties and a man's will decline. That should put you on about a level playing field with each other.

Lack of Leadership in the Home

Lots of women commented about men's lack of leadership in the home. Many men are too passive and apathetic in leading their families. There are a variety of reasons for this, some good and some not so good. I do know that a lot of men are good men and are working hard to be the best they can for their families.

This complaint is probably dependent on a number of factors. For instance, does his wife *allow* him to lead? Some women complain about a man's lack of leadership in the home but never let go of the reins long enough *for* him to lead. Does his wife criticize his attempts to lead? A man won't risk leading for long if all he gets is second-guessed whenever he makes a decision or criticized when he makes a mistake. Is his wife willing to follow? I've met some women who would absolutely not follow a man no matter how good a leader he was.

Sometimes we have to look deep within ourselves to recognize the things that irritate us most in others. Are you allowing your husband to lead in your home?

If you want to encourage your husband to lead in the home, you have to let him lead *his* way. Just know that his way will probably not be *your* way very often. He will probably be hesitant initially to lead. Your positive encouragement will be vital as he tentatively assumes a leadership role. Additionally, understand that if he has not been in a leadership role in the past, he cannot immediately take over all aspects of the position. He will need to take small steps over a period of time and become confident with his role and with your attitude regarding that role.

Bonus: The Toilet Seat

This doesn't really fit into a clear category but because so many women listed it as an irritant, I added it as a bonus annoyance. I'm not quite sure why this is such an issue, but as far as the whole toilet-seat-up-or-down topic goes, I've just never thought it was that big of a deal. I know it drives some (many . . . okay, all) women crazy, but I always thought, *I have to lift it up every time—what's the big deal about her having to lower it every time?*

When I asked my wife how she influenced the males in her home in these areas, she muttered something about "years of nagging and complaining . . ." as she walked by with a load of laundry. Seriously, though, I have made it a conscious effort to lower the toilet seat every time . . . but only recently. I initially started doing it because she complained about it and it was easier than getting nagged. But then I started doing it as a courtesy because I knew it would make her happy. I do it now because it is something that she wants and so it is a small way of honoring her. When I really stopped and thought about it, it was such a trivial thing. It's not that it was difficult or that I couldn't remember to do it if I really wanted to. Perhaps I was leaving it up as a way to aggravate her? Sort of a little passive-aggressive attempt to get back at her for something she was doing that bothered me. (By the way—those cute little signs above the toilet that remind men to lower the lid? They don't work.)

The obvious point to me was that, as she has learned over the years to meet my needs, I now *want* to do things that honor her and make her happy. I am conscious of those things (like putting the toilet seat down) that I was not before—probably because I was spending most of my waking hours thinking about how to get my own needs met.

It's worth a thought: if the toilet seat position and putting a fresh roll of toilet paper on the spool are the biggest problems you've got to complain about, maybe life is pretty good.

Ten Most Annoying Habits of Women

1. Interrupting great sports moments on TV.
2. Being moody and possessive.
3. Using our razor to shave her legs and armpits.
4. Not shaving her legs and armpits.
5. Complaining incessantly.
6. Speaking in code.
7. Overly emotional.
8. Always critical of other women.
9. Baby talk—enough said.
10. Tries on 500 different outfits and asks, "How do I look?"

Men are a bit of an enigma. They can accidentally cut their thumb off with a saw, pick it up, pack it in ice, and drive to the hospital without batting an eye. But let them try to change a poopy diaper and they start gagging and are rendered helpless.

As I reviewed the top complaints from women, most of the things on this list didn't seem all that important. Some were minor, albeit pretty annoying habits. But compared to utterly destructive behaviors such as infidelity, abusive behavior, addictions, financial malfeasance, compulsive lying, and slanderous behavior, these traits are minor aggravations in a relationship.

And, you know, women also have their little quirks that annoy guys.

Unfortunately, under the pressures of everyday life, these inconsequential items can snowball into big issues that damage a relationship. If you can look at the big picture in light of how these issues compare in significance to your overall relationship, you might recognize their relative place in the grand scheme of things.

Rather than majoring on the minors, sometimes it helps to activate your sense of humor or practice your ability to count to ten.

Recognizing that we cannot change other people and that we can only change ourselves, perhaps a change in perspective may help you deal with or understand some of these annoying behaviors. Maybe a man who provides for and protects his family but still occasionally leaves the toilet seat up deserves some slack. If your husband plays with the kids and is faithful to his wedding vows, maybe it's not so big a deal if he forgets to do a chore or wash the dishes from time to time.

Sometimes it's easy to concentrate only on the rock that's stuck in your shoe. If you stop and look at all the things your man *does* do for you instead of focusing on his faults, it's easier to remember that he really does work hard to try to make you happy. For the most part, your man is probably a pretty good man—that's why you married him. I suspect he often does not get as much credit as he deserves. In fact, it might be a good thing to make a list of the good qualities your husband possesses so you can review it from time to time. After all, it's easy to blame someone who can't or won't defend themselves very often. As one woman said, "I realized that I just needed to take a chill pill. I was blowing things way out of proportion to their significance."

The next time you feel angry or are about to go crazy at your man because of one of these Top Ten traits, take a deep breath and recite the following two prayers. Then count your blessings from God.

The Serenity Prayer

God grant me the serenity
to accept the things I cannot change;
courage to change the things I can;
and wisdom to know the difference.

Living one day at a time;
Enjoying one moment at a time;
Accepting hardships as the pathway to peace;
Taking, as He did, this sinful world
as it is, not as I would have it;
Trusting that He will make all things right
if I surrender to His Will;
That I may be reasonably happy in this life
and supremely happy with Him
Forever in the next.
Amen.

Reinhold Niebuhr

Trust in the LORD with all your heart
and lean not on your own understanding;
in all your ways acknowledge him,
and he will direct your paths.

Proverbs 3:5–6

10

Using Your Influence Effectively

Women hope men will change after marriage but they don't;
men hope women won't change but they do.

Bettina Arndt, *Private Lives*

Expectations often determine the success or failure of our
relationships. Many women enter a relationship thinking
that a man might have a few rough edges, but basically he is
good raw material to work with. Perhaps he drinks a few too
many beers or plays video games for hours on his computer,
but those are acceptable shortcomings considering the other
kinds of men available out there. She figures she can help mold
him into the best man he can be. Over the years, though, she
begins to get frustrated. He doesn't seem to want to change.
In fact, he resents and resists any efforts on her part to help
him be a better man.

Men enter into relationships with unrealistic expectations as well. For instance, he believes she is always going to be the physically beautiful, well-proportioned slip of a girl he married. But after a few years and a couple of kids take their toll, it is unrealistic to expect that a woman can maintain the same figure she had at twenty years of age. Men also enter into relationships with the expectation that regular sex will be a part of the deal. Additionally he thinks she will always be the agreeable, charming girl who went out of her way to serve him and anticipate his needs like the young girl he was dazzled by during courtship. He's frustrated by the fact that no matter what he does, she never seems satisfied. In fact, sometimes she's downright disagreeable. He's also a bit put off that she seems to want to change him. He thinks, *She married me the way I am, for crying out loud. Why does she want to change me?*

Given those divergent expectations, how can a woman use her influence in an honoring way to facilitate outside forces to encourage growth in her man? Also, what direct and indirect actions can she take that will benefit her man in his journey to significance?

Encourage Other Men in His Life

Men need other men. They communicate best with men. After all, it's kind of hard to joke about flatulence around women; for some reason they just don't seem to think it's funny. Let your man have male friends. It won't hurt your relationship. In fact, it will improve your relationship—provided he's around the *right* men. Hanging out with single guys is probably not a good idea.

The type of men he associates with plays a big influence on his attitude and mentality. If he surrounds himself with healthy men, he will grow and develop his character—the bar is set high. If he surrounds himself with unhealthy men, the bar is set low, and he will figure that by comparison he is pretty good and there's no need to change or grow. The unhealthy attitudes and behaviors of those men might also influence him into thinking certain behaviors are acceptable.

Good men also provide accountability. They will keep him from doing things he should not, and inspire him to engage in behaviors and attempt challenges that are good for him but that he wouldn't normally test himself with.

Men who are isolated from other men have no model to compare themselves against. Other men set the bar for them to compete against. Competition is a big part of a man's life. All men thrive in a spirit of competition. Even men who seem meek and mild yearn to pit themselves against other men in the heat of competition. I've had moms tell me their sons are bookish and not sports oriented and therefore are not competitive. But I've played chess against some of those "noncompetitive" boys, and they relished kicking my behind as quickly and ruthlessly as possible. I've also seen some musical competitions that were far more competitive than anything I've witnessed on the basketball court or football field. Even guys in the pastorate compete against their peers, if only in secret.

One way you can influence him into surrounding himself with good men is by intentionally going out of your way to develop relationships with the wives of good men. Men generally have a more difficult time making friends than women. Your skill in this area can smooth the way for him to establish relationships that he might normally be intimidated by.

Encourage Spiritual Leadership

Women are a bit mystical and quite possibly more spiritual than men are—at least, men think you are. Consequently, men are always a little confused and maybe even a little scared of women. You have that intuition thing going, and the whole moon and tide and monthly cycle thing is a little intimidating and mysterious to most men. Women also do a lot of things and use a lot of products that scare men. Your toiletries are a mystifying maze of complicated names and medieval-looking torture devices. Take eyelash curlers, for example. These utensils look like a device straight off the rack from a dungeon torture chamber. I envision some poor peasant chained to a rack screaming as his masked tormenter applies hot wax to his thighs while threateningly wielding eyelash curlers in front of his face.

Often women have a deeper faith in God than the average guy does. Frankly, the church does a poor job of capturing men's attention and inspiring them to greatness. Most men either don't go to church with their wives or else attend just to make her happy—but they are not actively engaged. Men are then expected to be spiritual leaders in their homes, yet we don't feel spiritually adequate ourselves and know we may not even be the most spiritual person in the household.

So given that perspective, how can a woman influence her man to be the spiritual leader in the home?

When I came to the Lord at the age of forty, I felt completely inadequate to be the spiritual leader in my home. I knew no Scripture, I could barely pray, and I didn't even know "Christian-ese," the lingo of faith. To make matters worse, every time I met with a group of my mature brothers (including pastors), I was always the one they asked to pray out loud. Talk about being intimidated!

However, my wife very gently insisted that I be the spiritual leader in our home. She urged me to take the lead even when I resisted. She always asked me to say grace at dinner and told the kids to come and ask me whenever they had a spiritual question. She did this with grace and faith. For instance, she never mentioned it when I got something wrong, and she always praised my efforts in front of the children. Even though she was probably a lot more spiritually mature than I, she allowed me to be the leader. *She did not expect me to be perfect, only that I would try my best.* That allowed me to make mistakes and learn from them without worrying about her correcting me or expecting me to do things the way she thought I should do them. Some women have expectations that the only *right* way to do something is the way they would do it. This generally sets men up in a no-win situation, as they seldom approach anything the same way a woman would.

My wife also encouraged me to be involved in activities that would help my spiritual growth. Most men are reluctant to attend a workshop or go away for a retreat weekend. Too often these kinds of events require us to be vulnerable, to sing, or even to hug someone. My attitude was, "I have too much to do around here, like mow the lawn, to attend a weekend retreat." However, she always pointed out how much I gained from the other activities I had attended. I would always find uplifting and honoring notes in my luggage when I did go away. Lastly, I always looked forward to her excited attitude and growing respect for me when I got home.

Those things encouraged me to pursue spiritual growth even when I was less than enthusiastic about making the effort.

Help Him Be a Better Dad

You have a great power to help your husband be a better father. And it's not by giving advice. Your encouragement is very influential in his fathering. In fact, you are the greatest asset he has as a father. You can provide him with information about the emotional lives and challenges of your children that he would not be aware of without your support.

Also, your edification of him as a father and leader in the home is hugely powerful in garnering the respect of his children. You can build him up in front of the children, gaining him respect that he couldn't garner on his own. When you show him respect and actively acknowledge his leadership, your children will as well. My wife severely scolded the kids any time they exhibited even the slightest amount of disrespect toward me.

But if you disrespect him, your children will probably not have much respect for him either. One woman I know frequently criticizes her husband in front of their children. While the kids love him, I'm not sure they respect him. The example their mother gives them is the example they follow.

Lastly, you are an excellent barometer to help him gauge how well he is doing as a father. He needs to know what the needs of his children are and when he does something well.

Dream with Your Husband

Being an average guy with a job, a wife, a mortgage, and 2.5 children can be a little boring. It often seems like all work and no play. All boys and young men grow up with dreams of glory and honor. They envision themselves as stars of the World

Series or heroes on the battlefield. They picture themselves overcoming impossible odds before, even though wounded and exhausted, they eventually, oh-so-gallantly win an epic battle between good and evil. Watch little boys at play as their imaginations run wild with the possibilities of life. Most of us never dreamed we would get old and end up as an accountant, a bank loan officer, or a hardware store owner. Since for many men what they do for a living is who they are, they often end up dissatisfied or frustrated with their lot in life. This has been the case for many years. In 1854, Henry David Thoreau alluded to this with his famous verse, "The mass of men lead lives of quiet desperation."

It's not that men don't enjoy and get fulfillment from their wives and children. It's just that most yearn for lives of significance—to be remembered for something other than how many cars they sold or loans they closed. The burdens and stresses of providing food, shelter, and the day-to-day necessities for a family can be daunting. The challenge becomes to find something that brings significance in what a man does—some goal or vision to work toward that inspires and inflames his passion.

Having a woman who encourages his dreams can fulfill that need for risk and adventure that all men possess, even if buried deep within their soul. But a woman who laughs at a man's dreams, calling them foolish or childish, causes him to stuff his need for release even deeper. Some men eventually become so desperate to release this need for "something they can't quite put their finger on but they know that this just can't be all that life is about," that they start making foolish choices and ruin their lives and the lives of those around them.

175

Ask him about his dreams. Encourage him to discover something he is passionate about. Ask him, "If time and money were no object, what would you want to spend the rest of your life doing?" Even if he never acts on his dreams, it is important for a man to have them.

Watch Out for His Health

Many men do not adequately take care of themselves all that well. So, when he is sick or has a medical problem, make sure he goes to the doctor. A lot of men either think it's a sign of weakness or are afraid to go to a doctor. I hate going to the doctor. Now that I've crossed the fifty-year-old barrier, all the tests and procedures they want to run seem pretty invasive. By gently insisting that he receive proper checkups and medical care, you are telling him you love him. He needs to know that you are concerned about what your life would be like if he were not around, and that you want him with you for a long time. He wants to know that you *need* him.

And when he's sick, he really needs you to nurture him. I know you think he's a baby, but sometimes a man does just need a little "mothering." A little tender loving care every now and then is a good remedy for what ails him.

Part of taking care of him is ensuring that he eats a healthy diet. As a general rule men will eat whatever is easiest and fastest to prepare, which often translates into fast food. Making sure he eats nutritious food is in the best interest of his long-term health. Even if he complains about it, he knows that you love and care about him.

Make sure he takes regularly scheduled time off from work. Men get focused on their work for a variety of reasons. First of all, he probably gets many more accolades through work than he does being a husband and father. Work also allows him to measure his accomplishments—whereas progress in relationships or parenting is often ambiguous and confusing.

Second, he is geared to derive his self-worth and self-image from work. He feels a sense of achievement through work. The better he does at his job, the better he feels about himself. His ability to provide well for his family is how he shows that he loves them. In ancient times, when a hunter returned home from a successful hunt, he was admired as a lifesaver. That action and response pattern has been bred into men over the generations.

Lastly, men were made to feel compelled to work. God commanded men to work until they die—but that this work would be difficult (in fact, it's actually a curse on him) (Gen. 3:19, 23). Men who work too long and too hard are subject to high levels of stress and even burnout. Stress can be very dangerous, causing a variety of symptoms and illnesses including heart disease, suppressed immune system, high blood pressure, depression, skin disorders, and decreased sex drive. Part of maintaining a healthy lifestyle is taking time off to relax and refresh yourself.

Regularly scheduled vacations and time away from work keep a man from falling into these health risks. Many men, unless coerced by a woman's influence, will not take time away from work because they have been programmed to feel either lazy or that they are not fulfilling their role if they are not working. A woman will help a man feel better about taking time off if she can make him understand that, while she appreciates his work efforts, she and the children want to spend time with him even more.

Pray with and for Your Husband

The greatest thing you can do for your man and your relationship is to pray. Women pray for a lot of things, especially their children, but many forget to focus on their husbands. Pray for him *every* day.

Pray for his work. He needs it to be productive and fulfilling to him. Work is a big part of his life. Work can fulfill or diminish him as a man. There's not much more discouraging for a man than working at an unfulfilling job he hates—especially if no one appreciates him for doing it.

Pray for the temptations he will face. He needs your help in this area. Before every seminar I present to women, Suzanne prays an extra hedge of protection around me—that no one will be sexually attracted to me and that I will not be tempted by any of the participants. She believes that her prayer as a wife has special power and influence in this area, and I tend to agree with her. Some women think it silly that another woman would ever be attracted to her husband. That is a very dangerous illusion to operate under. After all, *she* was attracted to him! The fact that my wife believes strongly enough that other women might be attracted to me that she asks for God's protection is also great for my self-esteem.

Men are also tempted almost daily with other issues besides sexual lust. Many men are in positions to be tempted to steal or cheat or compromise their principles. These are often small things that seem unimportant. But men seldom make a huge leap from being honorable to failing miserably. We do that by making small compromises until finally we find ourselves mired in a pit of sin and despair. For instance, men seldom make the huge leap from fidelity to adultery all at one time.

More often it is a series of small choices and compromises over a period of time that lead to his ultimate action of demise.

Pray for his wisdom and discernment. Besides eternal salvation, the greatest gift God gave to a man was that of great wisdom. Wisdom can help your husband in *every* aspect of his life. The best part is that the wiser your husband becomes, the more you reap the benefits.

The greatest spiritual growth that my wife and I have experienced, both separately and as a couple, came when we started praying together every day. This seems to be very difficult for most men. I know it was for me. Suzanne's eagerness and supportive attitude of the quality of my prayers inspires me to keep doing this even when I don't feel like it. It's my personal belief that this kind of spiritual teamwork by a husband and wife drives the evil one crazy. He will do anything to keep this from happening, so know that once you start praying together, it will take a concentrated effort by both of you to continue.

Lastly, *thank God for providing you with a good man.* Whatever his faults, your husband probably loves you so much he would be willing to give his life for you. There are not many people in the world who would make that kind of sacrifice for you. Be grateful for what you have—it will keep you focused on the positives in your relationship. Pray that the Lord would show you how best to love, nurture, and support your husband as part of a team. Ask God to bind you and your husband in a strong, satisfying marriage relationship.

⌒

Your husband needs your help in the areas I've described above. He needs a wife who partners with him and helps him be all the things he could not be without your presence. You deserve a husband who is authentically masculine—but he can only achieve this with your encouragement and influence. The actions I've described in this chapter can help boost your husband toward being the best man possible, maybe even toward greatness!

A Final Word

Women have the power to make the lives of those around them better just by their very presence. I know women whose influence with their families and those around them is phenomenal. They are using the influence God gave them in a manner that is life-giving to those they touch.

I've talked about men achieving greatness. Some women say, "My man is just an average guy; he could never be a *great* man." Well, maybe that's true—and it certainly will be if no one believes in him like only you can. He may never become great without your help and faith in him. Either way, he *will* fulfill whatever expectations you have of him. Every man has the seeds of greatness within him. They need to be watered and nurtured to grow. I believe that's a role God gave to you. But it's not easy—that role takes courage and persistence.

The man who is fortunate enough to walk beside a woman like this calls himself blessed. These women truly are women of influence. They have answered God's call to a higher standard in life—one of fulfilling their God-given role as helpmate and completer in a man's life. By living that role, they not only bless their husbands and children, but they themselves live lives of blessing, contentment, and great satisfaction.

And now you too know the key to becoming a Man Whisperer.

Notes

Chapter 1 A Woman's Whisper

1. Laura Schlessinger, *The Proper Care and Feeding of Husbands* (New York: Harper-Collins, 2004), xvi–xvii.

Chapter 2 Authentic Masculinity

1. Charles Colson with Harold Fickett, *The Good Life: Seeking Purpose, Meaning, and Truth in Your Life* (Wheaton: Tyndale House, 2005), 29, italics in original.

2. *Kingdom of Heaven*, directed by Ridley Scott (Twentieth Century-Fox Film, 2005).

3. Ernest Gordon, *To End All Wars* (Grand Rapids: Zondervan, 2002), 105–6.

4. Donald Miller and John MacMurray, *To Own a Dragon: Reflections on Growing Up without a Father* (Colorado Springs: NavPress, 2006), 139–40.

Chapter 4 Nine Traits That Hold Him Back

1. Excerpted from Gary and Merrilee Lewis, *Is He a Man or Just Another Guy? A Girl's Guide to Finding "Mr. Right"* (Bend, OR: GLO Publishing, 2002), 41–43.

2. Wikipedia, gleaned from definition of "passive-aggressive," http://en.wikipedia.org/wiki/Passive-aggressive_behavior.

3. Excerpted from Lewis, *Is He a Man or Just Another Guy?* 26.

4. James Lee Burke, *Crusader's Cross: A Dave Robicheaux Novel* (New York: Simon & Schuster, 2005), 174.

5. National Coalition Against Domestic Violence, 1992, as quoted in Patricia Riddle Gaddis, *Dangerous Dating: Helping Young Women Say No to Abusive Relationships* (Colorado Springs: Waterbrook, 2000), 44.

6. Department of Justice, "Bureau of Justice Statistics: National Crime Victimization Survey", Washington, DC, August 1995.

7. Angela Thomas, *Do You Think I'm Beautiful? The Question Every Woman Asks* (Nashville: Thomas Nelson, 2003), 178.

Chapter 5 Speaking Your Man's Language

1. Michael Gurian, *The Wonder of Boys* (New York: Jeremy P. Tarcher/Putnam Books, 1996), 14–15.

2. Florence Littauer, *After Every Wedding Comes a Marriage* (Eugene, OR: Harvest House, 1981), adapted from pp. 168–76.

3. "Differences Between Men and Women," Relationship Institute, http://www .relationship-institute.com/freearticles_detail.cfm?article_ID=151.

4. Frank Pittman, *Man Enough: Fathers, Sons and the Search for Masculinity* (New York: G. P. Putnam's Sons, 1993), 248.

5. John T. Molloy, *Why Men Marry Some Women and Not Others* (New York: Warner, 2003), 124.

Chapter 7 The First Man in Every Woman's Life

1. Lois Mowday, *Daughters Without Dads: Offering Understanding and Hope to Women Who Suffer from the Absence of a Loving Father* (Nashville: Oliver-Nelson Books, 1990), 64.

2. Ibid.

3. Ibid., 60.

4. Victoria Secunda, *Women and Their Fathers: The Sexual and Romantic Impact of the First Man in Your Life* (New York: Delacorte Press, 1992), 211.

5. Thomas, *Do You Think I'm Beautiful?* 52.

6. Frank Pittman, quoted in Secunda, *Women and Their Fathers*, 402–3.

7. Ibid., xvi.

Chapter 8 Sex Is *Not* a Weapon

1. Stephen Aerterburn, Fred Stoecker with Mike Yorkey, *Every Man's Battle: Winning the War on Sexual Temptation One Victory at a Time* (Colorado Springs: WaterBrook, 2000), 63.

2. Kevin Leman, *Making Sense of the Men in Your Life: What Makes Them Tick, What Ticks You Off, and How to Live in Harmony* (Nashville: Thomas Nelson, 2000), 130.

3. Shaunti Feldhahn, *For Women Only: What You Need to Know about the Inner Lives of Men* (Sisters, OR: Multnomah, 2004), 92.

4. Ibid., 92–93.

5. Barbara Defoe Whitehead and David Popenoe, "The State of Our Unions: Why Men Won't Commit—Exploring Young Men's Attitudes about Sex, Dating and Marriage," The National Marriage Project, Rutgers University, Piscataway, NJ, 2002, 6–7.

6. Sharon Sassler, professor of sociology, Ohio State University, and James McNally, Institute for Social Research, University of Michigan, study published in *Social Science Research*. Jeff Grabmeier, "Cohabiting Couples Not Likely to Marry, Study Finds," Ohio State Research News, http://researchnews.osu.edu/archive/cohabit.htm.

7. Whitehead and Popenoe, "The Status of Our Unions," 11.

Chapter 9 The Top Ten Things about Men That Drive Women Crazy

1. Sue Shellenbarger, "Men Do More Housework Than Women Think," Wall Street Journal Online, http://www.careerjournal.com/columnists/workfamily/20050520-workfamily.html.

2. Lisa Sullivan, Margaret Kelly-Hayes, Emelia J. Benjamin, and Ralph B. D'Agostino, "Non-traditional roles may boost risk of heart disease and death," American Heart Association website, 4/24/02, http://www.americanheart.org/presenter.jhtml?identifier=3002344.

3. William Pollack, *Real Boys* (New York: Henry Holt & Co., 1998), 5.

4. John Gray, *Mars and Venus Together Forever* (New York: HarperPerennial, 1994), 119.

Author and speaker **Rick Johnson** founded Better Dads, a fathering skills program, based on the urgent need to empower men to lead and serve in their families and communities. Rick's books have expanded his ministry to include influencing the whole family, with life-changing insights for men and women on parenting, marriage, and personal growth. He is a sought-after speaker at many large conferences across the US and Canada and is a popular keynote speaker at men's and women's retreats and conferences on parenting and marriage. Additionally, he is a nationally recognized expert in several areas, including the effects of fatherlessness, having been asked to deliver papers at various venues.

To find out more about Rick Johnson, his books, and the Better Dads ministry, or to schedule workshops, seminars, or speaking engagements, please visit www.betterdads.net

Meet

RICK JOHNSON

at www.BetterDads.net

Connect with Rick on Facebook
Rick Johnson

YOUR RECIPE FOR MARITAL SUCCESS

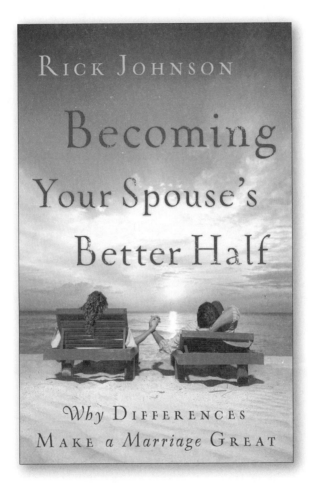

Learn how to use your differences to add spice and passion to your marriage.

Revell
a division of Baker Publishing Group
www.RevellBooks.com

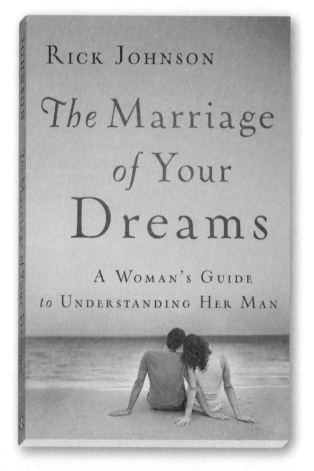

Encouragement and advice for moms from family expert

RICK JOHNSON

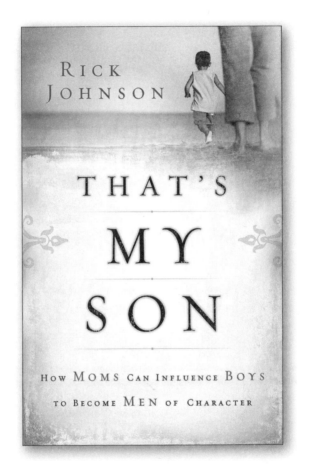

RICK
JOHNSON

THAT'S

MY

SON

HOW MOMS CAN INFLUENCE BOYS
TO BECOME MEN OF CHARACTER

A mother's imprint on her son lasts *forever*.

ENCOURAGEMENT FOR FATHERS IN THEIR MOST IMPORTANT ROLE

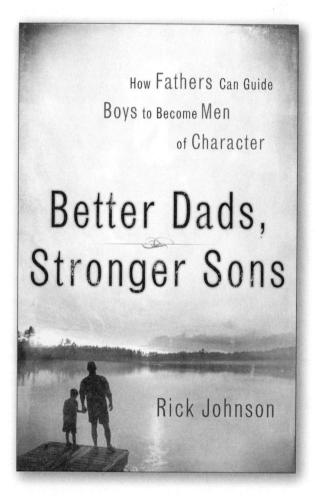

How Fathers Can Guide
Boys to Become Men
of Character

Better Dads, Stronger Sons

Rick Johnson

 Revell
a division of Baker Publishing Group
www.RevellBooks.com

Available Wherever Books Are Sold
Also Available in Ebook Format